D0966696

MODERN LATIN AMERICAN NARRATIVES

MODERN LATIN AMERICAN NARRATIVES

The Dreams of Reason

Alfred J. Mac Adam

The University of Chicago Press
Chicago and London

The University of Chicago Press,
Chicago 60637
The University of Chicago Press, Ltd.,
London

© 1977 by the University of Chicago
All rights reserved. Published 1977
Printed in the United States of America

81 80 79 78 77   987654321

Library of Congress Cataloging in Publication Data

Mac Adam, Alfred J 1941–
    Modern Latin American narratives.

    Bibliography: p.
    1. Latin American fiction—History and criticism—
Addresses, essays, lectures.   2. Satire, Latin American—
History and criticism—Addresses, essays, lectures.
I.   Title.
PQ7082.N7M27   863'.009   76-8098
ISBN 0-226-49993-6

ALFRED J. MAC ADAM is associate
professor in the Department of Spanish and Portuguese at Yale University. He is the author of *El individuo y
el otro: Crítica a los cuentos de Julio
Cortázar*.

*To June and Leonard Stone,
my mother- and father-in-law,
in appreciation for all they
have done for me*

e parve di costoro quelli che vince,
non colui che perde.

Contents

Acknowledgements

I would like to express my gratitude to the Morse Fellowship committee of Yale University for granting me the time to finish this text. I would also like to thank, respectively, Professor Karl-Ludwig Selig of Columbia University for having printed, in *Revista Hispánica Moderna,* an early version of my essay on Manuel Puig, and Professor Alfredo Roggiano of the University of Pittsburgh for having published an early version of my essay on Guillermo Cabrera Infante in *Revista Iberoamericana.*

Special thanks are due to friends at Yale whose advice enabled me to make sense of my own ideas. These include A. Bartlett Giamatti, Paul H. Fry, and Emir Rodríguez Monegal.

To my wife, Barbara, I owe much more than I can ever hope to express.

Introduction

Latin American Narrative & Literary Genres

This study examines a limited number of Latin American narratives, all published within the last ninety or so years, in an attempt to determine the distinctive features of what may seem to be a literary chaos. The study seeks to determine the common elements lying at the core of these texts by ascertaining the genre in which most of them are written. Since the subject of the essay is literature, not literature and society or literature and philosophy, extraliterary matters will be referred to only as adjuncts to literary speculation. "Final causes" for literary phenomena will be drawn from the juxtaposition of Latin American texts and their Western counterparts, so that Latin American narrative may be seen as a part of the Western literary tradition, not as a *lusus naturae*.

However, because Latin American writing is the product of a colonial society, one manifestly influenced by metropolitan centers,[1] it must be studied in a double perspective. These texts cannot be understood either on exclusively native or exclusively comparative grounds because they are the result of a fusion of both worlds. It is possible to speak of the "Victorian novel" because of the literary and cultural homogeneity of Victoria's reign—though it might make more sense to speak of the nineteenth-century novel in less national terms—but there is no unified body of writing from any single Latin American country during any historical period (and this would include the so-called novel of the Mexican Revolution) which would recapitu-

late all the concerns of the entire continent. There is no single
national literature in Latin America that captures the "spirit of
the age" for the rest of Latin America.

At the same time, to divest these texts of their local resonance
is equally impossible. For example, critics have tried to deal with
Jorge Luis Borges[2] as if he were a man without a country. However, Borges's nationality must be taken into account if his work
is to be appreciated to the fullest; no matter how cosmopolitan
his stories seem, there is an Argentine sensibility present in all
of them. And what is true of Borges is certainly true of the
writers presented here.

But even if these texts are read in the double light of local
tradition and comparative literature, they often elude comprehension because they are read according to a rhetoric alien to
them. What is called the Latin American novel is, according to
the definitions set out here, not a novel at all. There is no Latin
American novel, following our understanding of the term, but
there is a Latin American satire. It is the intention of this essay to
demonstrate why the extended narrative writing of Latin
America is satire (or, rarely, romance), and why it is imperative
that these texts be read according to a rhetoric based on satire
and not on the novel. To accomplish this it will be necessary to
define terms, forge taxonomies, and show how the misuse of
critical terms leads to misreading.

Such a study requires a consideration of genre theory, a much
debated and belabored subject. The soundest approach to this
Gordian knot has been expressed by William K. Wimsatt:

> It's the same as the logical problem whether we can describe
> an individual. As soon as we start describing him we have to
> classify him. And what the literary critic says, I think, on that
> score is that each literary work is unique, individual, but that
> as far as we attempt to analyze it or describe it, we put it in
> classes and we don't hope to exhaust it.[3]

The utilization of literary genres as an approach to Latin American narrative fiction is not therefore an end in itself, but a
means, a way of reading according to the rhetorical intentions of
the texts themselves.

While much speculation on the concept of literary genres has

been written since Aristotle discussed tragedy, comedy, and
epic, recent work has added significantly to making the relationships between readers and genres and between genres themselves more coherent. Two critics, E. D. Hirsch and Northrop
Frye,[4] have made important contributions along these lines, and
it seems fitting to review some of their ideas. Hirsch places the
problem of genres squarely on the reader himself when he postulates his idea of "intrinsic genres": *"It is that sense of the whole by
means of which an interpreter can correctly understand any part in its
determinacy"* (Hirsch, p. 86, italics in original). Linguistics
teaches that for communication to take place, speakers must
share a code; similarly, an author, who invents neither language
nor literature, utilizes certain extant models when he writes. His
use of those models is his interpretation of his literary tradition,
and it seems logical to suggest that new genres are the result of
personal interpretations of genres already in use. The reader-
interpreter, if we extrapolate from Wimsatt's remark, must relate the particular work at hand to his own literary code, fit it
into his range of literary possibilities. The idea of the intrinsic
genre teaches us that writing and reading are parallel but different activities: In the first, the author's ideas are translated
through writing into a totality which is both old and new. It is
related to experience and education in that it uses (however
ironically) models already in existence, and it is unique in that
no other translation of tradition blended with personal interpretation is quite like it. The reader reverses this process by first
associating, as far as experience and education will permit, the
text with other texts he sees as similar, and then savoring the
individual interpretation of those givens.

When Hirsch says that "every shared type of meaning (every
intrinsic genre) can be defined as a system of conventions"
(Hirsch, p. 92), we realize how much depends on all parties
being aware that conventions of this sort do exist. He warns
against the use of genres as a means to define a literature, as it
were, from without: "any heuristic type idea which an interpreter applied to a great many different utterances would be ex-
trinsic if it were not narrowed in a different way for different
utterances" (Hirsch, p. 88). Again, in a note to the same passage:
"Thus my objection to the dangerous practice of using abstract

categories or monolithic 'approaches' and 'methods' to interpret a wide variety of texts. The use of such master keys to unlock large numbers of texts often has the effect of fitting the lock to the key rather than vice versa" (Hirsch, pp. 88–89). We must realize how important it is to fight the misuse of certain genre designations by means of a wider use of certain other terms. The case in point is the by now meaningless designation *novel* for virtually any book longer than one-hundred and fifty pages. If it is possible to get to the essence of the narrative fiction of Latin America, it will be by means of a reading aimed at a generalized or inductive form of the intrinsic genre (*malgré* Hirsch's misgivings). To translate that abstracted intrinsic genre into practical critical language, to make it useful as a heuristic tool— something Latin American literature lacks—it is necessary to associate the intrinsic genre with one of the genre designations already in common use. And to make it work, the term will have to be tinkered with again and again so that it will be "narrowed in a different way for different utterances" while it retains its abstract sense. That is, a reading of the works considered in this essay would leave the reader aware of a unity within diversity. The aim of this study is to examine that unity and give it a name.

It is in Northrop Frye's fourth essay in the *Anatomy of Criticism*, "Rhetorical Criticism: Theory of Genres," that the genres are defined in such a way that it is possible to compare them, to see how each reflects the others, how reading without a knowledge of these conventions is practically impossible. Frye finds the origin of genre distinctions in what he calls the "radical of presentation": "Words may be acted in front of a spectator; they may be spoken in front of a listener; they may be sung or chanted; or they may be written for a reader" (Frye, p. 247). That someone might read a play instead of seeing it acted, or read a poem instead of hearing it recited is not an important factor in determining the radical of presentation because the mode is significant purely as an indicator of which tradition the present work is meant to evoke. As we read, for example, Trollope's *Barchester Towers* or Machado de Assis's *Memórias Póstumas de Brás Cubas*, we are aware that although the texts were destined for individual, silent readers, their chatty narrators push the works toward Frye's "epos," "works in which the radical of presentation is oral address" (Frye, p. 248).

Making a distinction strikingly similar to the one Jakobson makes between metaphor and metonymy in *Fundamentals of Language*,[5] Frye first distinguishes between *epos*, the rhythm of recurrence typical of poetry, and the rhythm of prose, which "is continuous, not recurrent" (Frye, p. 263). For the purposes of this study, the mode of recurrence will be referred to as *metaphor* and the mode of continuance will be termed *metonymy*; deciding first which of these predominates in a given text provides the initial basis for deciding with which texts to associate the one under scrutiny. The importance of this seemingly elementary distinction will be seen later (chapter 12) in the comparison of two works which deal with the artist's life: one the life of the narrator, in which metonymy is the basic mode, and the other the life of the poet, in which metaphor predominates.

Frye finds four principal types of prose fiction: novel, confession, anatomy, and romance. It might be judicious to give his definitions of these forms and then to show how they will be modified for the purposes of this essay. After comparing novel and romance, and noting that the novel "tends to expand into a fictional approach to history" (Frye, p. 306), Frye concludes:

> The novel tends to be extroverted and personal; its chief interest is in human character as it manifests itself in society. The romance tends to be introverted and personal: it also deals with characters, but in a more subjective way. (Subjective here refers to treatment, not subject-matter. The characters of romance are heroic and therefore inscrutable; the novelist is freer to enter his characters' minds because he is more objective.) The confession is also introverted, but intellectualized in content. (Frye, p. 308)

Frye's definition of satire (a term he replaces with *anatomy* but which shall be retained here) also begins with a meditation on character:

> The Menippean satire deals less with people as such than with mental attitudes. Pedants, bigots, cranks, parvenus, virtuosi, enthusiasts, rapacious and incompetent professional men of all kinds, are handled in terms of their occupational approach to life as distinct from their social behavior. The

> Menippean satire thus resembles the confession in its ability
> to handle abstract ideas and theories, and differs from the
> novel in its characterization, which is stylized rather than
> naturalistic, and presents people as mouthpieces of the ideas
> they represent.... The novelist sees evil and folly as social
> diseases, but the Menippean satirist sees them as diseases of
> the intellect. (Frye, p. 309)

We may conclude from these observations that Frye bases his
genre determinations on what he calls the "radical of presentation," on character, and on the author's attitude toward time.
This study is in general agreement with this means of determining the genre of a given text, but would add a few details.

First, the idea of temporal design: Time in Frye's understanding of the novel is indeed, as he suggests, "a fictional approach
to history," but it is an attitude toward a particular kind of
history, history seen in dialectical terms. It is helpful to fuse
some of the ideas of Georg Lukács[6] with those of Frye in order to
define the novel as that genre which studies the psychological
development of characters whose lives are linked with specific
sides in the dialectical battleground of history. If we view the
novel in this way we can see how it uses history as a dynamic
background for the lives of its characters whereas historical data
appear in the satire or in romance as static backdrops against
which a *psychomachia* is played. This distinction is of crucial importance for Latin American narrative because a Hegelian attitude toward history never shapes its plots. That is, the essential characteristic of the novel, its historiographic core, is absent
in Latin American fiction.

This nondialectical or nonevolutionary attitude toward history
may be (extrapolating from the Steins' work) a reflection of the
realities of colonial life itself, although it is not the intention of
this essay to draw such (unprovable in any case) conclusions.
What is true, however, (and here we return to Hirsch's intrinsic
genres) is that in none of the texts examined here is there a
dialectical concept of history. There may be a cyclical attitude, as
there is in Gabriel García Márquez's *Cien años de soledad*; there
may be an idea of history as a series of repetitions, as there is in
João Guimarães Rosa's *Grande Sertão: Veredas*; but for the most

part there is the presentation of characters who are explored as types against a backdrop that would be more or less familiar to the readers in terms of names and artifacts (very few texts resort to gross exoticism or overtly allegorical settings). The setting as a temporal reality is presented as unchanging and radically separate from the destinies of the characters themselves, who stand primarily as figures in a landscape instead of beings intimately connected to the temporal changes in the setting.

Along with its different attitude toward history, the satire differs from the novel in its decorum. Satire is the genre of excesses, of the unleashing of energies repressed either by the novel's faith in history or in the romance's faith in archetypes. It is this will to overload the narrative with information or with grotesque exaggerations that also separates the satire from the confession, which strives toward some metaphor of unity through time.[7] That the satires of Machado de Assis studied here are also written in the confessional mode does not alter this conclusion: the first person, autobiographical stance constitutes the "radical of presentation," but what the text is "about" is not the self but an idea.

This last factor we may call the text's dominant metaphor. If we agree that all narratives are metaphoric in one way or another, we may see how the kind of metaphor that predominates in a given text links it to one genre or another. The idea of *mimesis* or imitation is itself a metaphor for the idea of metaphor: imitation may be seen either as an association of activities or as the substitution of one kind of activity for another. A novel is metaphoric in that it presents what is to be construed as a picture of real life, even if that picture is essentially a synecdoche, a selection of elements which constitutes a totality. Satire has a different sort of metaphoric background. It substitutes one set of metaphors for another, dealing with what are already general qualities; in fact, even if a real person is parodied in a satire, he is promptly shorn of his real identity because he is blended with a stereotype. It is for this reason that the plot of satire tends to be elastic, paratactic, and monstrously disproportionate: the scene displaces the whole, and the collision of abstract entities takes place in concentrated bursts rather than in the extended, de-

velopmental plots of other forms. Romance also tends to be
metaphor about metaphor as accretions are added by cultures
and individuals to a handful of archetypal stories.

When we speak of literary genres we are dealing, as Hirsch
reminds us, with conventions, with working hypotheses that
enable us to deal with groups of texts instead of texts taken in
isolation. To speak of genres is to admit that works are depend-
ent on one another and that while authors are individuals, their
works inevitably display certain family traits. Built into the concept of literary genres is one irresolvable problem: do the generic
terms have a significance that is purely historical, or do they
transcend historical periods? That is, are the genres bound to a
specific moment in cultural history, as the young Lukács seemed
to think? He says, in *Theory of the Novel* (1920):

> Artistic genres now cut across one another, with a complexity
> that cannot be disentangled, and become traces of authentic
> or false searching for an aim that is no longer clearly and
> unequivocally given; their sum total is only a historical total-
> ity of the empirical, wherein we may seek (and possibly find)
> the empirical (sociological) conditions for the ways in which
> each form came into being, but where the historico-
> philosophical meaning of periodicity is never again con-
> centrated in the forms themselves (which have become sym-
> bolic) and where this meaning can be deciphered and de-
> coded from the totalities of various periods, but not discov-
> ered in those totalities themselves.[8]

Whether (in the Saussurean sense) the genres are synchronic or
diachronic concepts, whether they are entities which have a
history (with origins, development, and death), or whether they
are Platonic ideals, are all problems that defy resolution. Because of this, one is tempted to regard Lukács' history-bound
view of the genres as a distortion of genre theory. The literary
text exists before someone (other than the author) attempts to
designate it as belonging to a particular genre. Its generic identity
begins only when it is compared with other texts, at which point
the historical context in which it first appeared ceases to be of
great significance, since it is the text as a verbal artifact (not as
historical phenomenon or reflection of a historical moment) that
is under scrutiny.

For Latin American literary criticism, a weak tradition in most countries, the absence of genre study has opened the way to critical fragmentation and the spontaneous generation of jargon. For example, critics have been convinced that Julio Cortázar's *Rayuela* contains a new esthetics of narrative when in fact Cortázar has simply given new names to old phenomena. Cortázar, one of the most prominent members of the so-called Boom[9] of the Latin American "novel," has always used literary criticism as a way of defining his own literary preoccupations.[10] He continuously creates imaginary obstacles to creation, Royal Academies of the mind, which he attacks and destroys in his literary works. In *Rayuela* the enemy is something called the "traditional novel," which can only be defeated by the invention of an "antinovel," which is presumably what *Rayuela* is. What Cortázar really did was to write in another, preexistent genre he assumed to be an "antinovel."[11] Cortázar's esthetic musings are interesting because of what they reveal about him, but they do not help the prospective reader of Latin American narrative at all. Such concepts as "antinovel" and critical techniques which double our confusion by hyphenating the word novel to produce the "new-novel," the "catholic-novel," the "picaresque-novel," are drawing criticism into a relativistic territory where everything is a novel and the word novel means nothing.

Latin American satire includes texts like *Rayuela* which define themselves as heterodox, texts which consistently run against the grain. Books such as Donoso's *El obsceno pájaro de la noche* or Sarduy's *De donde son los cantantes* embody the melange idea implied in the word *"satura."*[12] And others, like Adolfo Bioy Casares's *Plan de evasión* or Machado de Assis' *Memórias Póstumas de Brás Cubas*, confound the reading process because they are hodge-podge texts in which part conflicts with part, in which character is indistinguishable from idea, in which plot is fragmented, and in which the local and the universal are bedfellows. Latin American satire is a carnival literature, a world-turned-upside-down literature, combining the Western literary tradition with the cultural contradictions of Latin America.

1

Machado de Assis
Satire & Madness

A narrative is the deployment of words to represent the passage of time. It is of no consequence whether the temporal flow is circular or linear; all narratives are committed to time, which is of their essence. But there is also built into narrative, into words used as narration, a contrary activity, one that concentrates the reader's attention on a timeless moment. These two notions, derived from the notions of synchrony and diachrony in Saussure's linguistics,[1] constitute the basic structure of all narratives. Furthermore, they may be seen as identical to the distinctions Jakobson makes between metaphor and metonymy in *Fundamentals of Language:* "The development of a discourse may take place along two different semantic lines: one topic may lead to another either through their similarity or through their contiguity. The METAPHORIC way would be the most appropriate term for the first case and the METONYMIC way for the second, since they find their most condensed expression in metaphor and metonymy respectively" (p. 90). While metaphor (or selection) and metonymy (or combination) are the basis of all discourse, one tends to predominate in the various sorts of literary discourse. As we have already seen in Frye, poetry tends toward "epos" or recurrence, while prose tends toward continuance and flow: what we shall see in the works examined in this essay is the conflict between metaphor and metonymy, between closure and extension, between synchrony and diachrony.

When we consider Machado de Assis's *Memórias Póstumas de*

Brás Cubas (1881) in the light of this opposition, we find the conflict first expressed as a struggle between the flow of life and the metaphorizing tendency of autobiography. This is the problem of unity in any first person narrative, the one Don Quijote presents to Ginés de Pasamonte (*Don Quijote*, bk. 1, chap. 22): how can a picaresque narrative end—that is, have unity—unless the life of the *pícaro* is over. Machado resolves this difficulty by locating his narrator outside of time, in eternity. From the privileged vantage point of death, to which, presumably, the past conceals no secrets, Brás presents the reader with the events that constitute his life. To prove he will have no difficulty finishing his story, Brás begins by describing his death: "Life was shuddering within my breast with the power of an ocean wave, awareness faded, I sank into physical and moral immobility, and my body became vegetable, stone, mud, nothing" (p. 512/20–21).[2] This passage marks a moment in Machado's literature in which he is consciously liberating himself from the resolutions to certain narrative problems presented to him by his immediate literary tradition. First, the narrator makes us see that it will be impossible for us to identify ourselves with him. That is, he demands that we never forget either his fictional identity or his being "on the other side" of time. All writers of autobiographies, as Olney points out, claim some sort of special point of view with regard to their own lives, and it is one of the standard fixtures of the Spanish picaresque that the hero comment on himself, as he was, as if that other self were dead. Here however we find no such ethical posturing; the difference between the narrator's two selves is the relationship each has to time.[3]

The ramifications of this temporal status for determining the text's genre are serious. An omniscient narrator can tell things about which the characters themselves are ignorant; character-narrators, located simultaneously within and beyond the action they describe, can reveal things they themselves do not suspect. But both of these types of narrator exist primarily as shapers of temporal flow. Their purpose is to organize linear narrative into a particular shape. Brás Cubas, to be sure, does exactly this, but he does it in such a way, from such an alien perspective, that we must consider what he says not only as flow but also as icon, not only as metonymic narrative flow but also as metaphor.

When we say that a text is metaphoric, that it has, in Jakobson's sense, drifted away from metonymic scene linking, we are admitting that the text is discourse à propos of something else. It is of the nature of satire and romance to be accumulations of metaphors: the great problem of interpreting metaphoric texts involves locating the referent, the meaning which would "close" the open gap of metaphor. This, clearly, is impossible, and it is the peculiar nature of metaphor, of all signs in fact, to be eternally elusive, always suggesting something which they can never be.

Brás Cubas, from his first words, knows what he is doing, and he explains why he is doing it by confessing a life-long desire for fame and glory. He hopes to gain immortality, after death, by writing a text, and in doing so renders ironic a traditional apology for writing. The text will be his life story, his autobiography, but a reading of the book reveals that it can in no way be taken for an exemplary life. The saint's life is a model to be emulated: even Saint Augustine offers himself as an example, implying that what happened to him can happen to the reader. The lives of great men are called "inspirational" precisely because they spur the reader on to imitate the hero's life. Brás Cubas falls into neither category, unless we think of him as we would of Lazarillo De Tormes, as a negative saint whose ironic life is a model to be avoided rather than copied. Of course, Lazarillo, unlike Brás, spends his life trying not to be what he is, trying to find his place in the world. Brás's life is as ironic as Lazarillo's, the difference being one of emphasis: Brás is spiritually dead amidst material comfort, while Lazarillo must die spiritually in order to achieve material comfort.

Brás's tale is certainly as pessimistic as Lazarillo's, but the ethical impetus behind Lazarillo's story, its criticisms of institutions and people, is lacking in Brás's memoirs. The institutions with which Lazarillo collides do not have the same weight in Brás's narrative: he envisions society as composed of greedy egoists, but he does not suggest, as Lazarillo's narrative does, that human affairs might be bettered if institutions were reformed. This concept, common in the didactic satires of the eighteenth century, is alien to the text, probably because the naturalists of the same era—and many texts by Machado's Portuguese counterpart, Eça de Queiroz (1845–1900)—were criticisms of society with an eye toward its regeneration.

Society in Brás's book is a projection of man himself; therefore it contains the same bizarre mixture of ideals and perversities as its creator. If Brás is a pessimist, it is not because he is horrified by man as a social animal, but because he sees life as a series of futile exercises leading to an end identical for the good and the bad, the foolish and the wise. Brás is a pessimist, not on an ethical or social level, but on a biological level. To act, to be idle, to move, or to stand still often turn out to be synonyms instead of antonyms. When Brás strives for something, for Virgília the woman he loves, for example, he loses. Later she becomes his mistress without his having to fight at all. That this is a parody of Augustinian grace may be true, but it is certain that whatever man's plans may be, they lead inexorably to the grave. Antiexistentialist from the outset, Brás's discourse mocks even itself: his is a voice from the grave telling us we have nothing to lose.

In the perspective of the ideologically "committed" literature of the same era, from the point of view of naturalism, for example, Machado's text is reactionary. Its radical skepticism, which discredits all notions of progress and history, and all hopes of altering human nature, runs contrary to the spirit of the age, but not, of course, to the spirit of satire. Just as he had done in his first extended narrative, *Ressurreição* (1872),[4] Machado extracts his protagonist from the "struggle for life," releasing him thereby from any involuntary contact with the world around him. It is in this liberation of the protagonist from the world of contingencies that we see Machado's desire to present his subject as an ethical or psychological type rather than as a "real" person living in a real world.

It is in this attitude that we see Machado turning away from a representation of time as history, metonymical realism (in Jakobson's sense), and turning toward the presentation of time as metaphorical scene. The "free form of a Sterne, or of a Xavier de Maistre," that Brás posits as a model in his first paragraph is in reality not free at all, but an abandonment of plot as an imita-

tion or metaphor of history. Machado's work proceeds by accumulation, in the same way Lazarillo's does, and it is in this
subjective sorting that we see the author turning toward satire.
We may wonder why Brás thinks of Sterne and de Maistre—he
is presumably referring to *Tristram Shandy*, *The Sentimental Journey*, and *Voyage autour de ma chambre*[5]—as utilizing a free form,
and we may simultaneously ask what texts he would think of as
not being "free." It would seem that freedom for Brás is the
ability to digress, to abandon plot, while the opposite, keeping
to a linear flow and adhering to a plot, constitutes imprison-
ment. And yet this seems too vague a distinction. *Tristram
Shandy* has a plot, its own particular kind, and it would seem
that Brás's story also possesses one. The type of plot neither has
is one based on history, on a Hegelian concept of history which
postulates a goal in the historical process.

Nothing typifies Machado's attitude toward history better
than the celebrated chapter 7, "Delirium." Brás begins the chapter with another "first" (he is already the first dead man to
become an author): he will describe his own delirium. But this
mental disorder is peculiarly iconic in its development. It begins
with a series of metamorphoses by the subject himself: he becomes a Chinese barber and a morocco-bound edition of the
Summa Theologica before returning to his own shape. Both of
these seemingly bizarre transformations may be images of the
artist—the barber who shaves a capricious mandarin, who
punishes and rewards his servant at the same time, and the text
which is the writer once he has died or ceased to exercise any
control over it. Neither of these interpretations is far-fetched
when we think of Kafka's hunger-artist, who starves himself to
entertain his public, or Borges's "Borges and I" (1960),[6] where
the living author acknowledges that the Borges whose name
appears on the spine of books, who is somehow different from
the man who lives in Buenos Aires, is "more real" than he is.
The portrait of the artist is in fact the most consistent motif in the
texts under consideration in this study.

The problem of universal history enters the chapter when
Brás, in his own shape, is whisked away to the "origin of the
centuries" by a hippopotamus. There would seem to be at least
three other literary texts in the background of the scene: the

Divine Comedy, an influence which pervades all of Machado's work; *Gulliver's Travels*, especially the scenes with the Brobding-nagians; and Camões's *Os Lusiadas*, particularly the Adamastor episode. Machado's relationship with Dante is a complex matter, but in *Memórias Póstumas* the *Commedia* may be seen as an ironic analogue to what Machado's text is. Dante, in life, is granted a trip to the tripartite other world, and is then told to publish his vision. Symbolically, he dies and is resurrected so that he may die and again be raised, this last time for eternity. His text is a message of hope for all Christians, but unlike Saint Augustine's, it gives testimony to a miracle, something more spectacular than an individual's receiving grace.

Brás is mad (delirious) when he has his vision (his madness is the result of illness, however, not divine inspiration), and his experience is a kind of affirmation of the nothingness which awaits him and has awaited all those who came before. There is no hope in Nature's (or Pandora's, the female figure who in-structs Brás) message to Brás; the only hope she bears is the one nurtured by all men, a hope which is naturally fatuous. Unlike Dante, who also visits the "origin of the centuries" when he enters the Earthly Paradise in *Purgatory* 28, Brás is presented with a vision of the centuries in the form of an endless parade of identical beings: all the ages of mankind are one in ethical terms and all pursue a Harlequin-like figure:

> a nebulous and fleeting figure, made of bits and pieces, a bit of the intangible, a piece of the improbable, a bit of the invisi-ble, all sewn loosely together with the needle of imagination; and that figure, nothing less than the chimera of happiness, either fled perpetually or let itself be caught by its skirt, and the one who caught it would grasp it to his breast while the figure would laugh in mockery and disappear like an illusion. (P. 521/35)

Both happiness and hope are verbal fictions, like Brás's vision, and exist only as figments of the imagination.

Brás's Nature/Pandora, a colossal female figure combining as-pects of the Brobdingnagians, of Adamastor, and of Baudelaire's giantess, is a grotesque. She is a kind of eternal feminine, a parody of both Matelda and Beatrice, anthropomorphic but not human, whose sole function is to show man (Brás) an objective picture of the universe. She gives no explanations, makes no promises, instills no hopes: she *is*, and her existence, together with the spectacle of the procession of the ages, all set in an ice-bound wasteland "beyond Eden" instead of a garden, moves Brás to see the insignificance of human life.

In a sense, Brás's delirium vision, an echo of the Erasmian blend of reason and folly, represents a systematic negation of the transcendental significance assigned to space in the *Divine Comedy*. Dante begins his journey on a plane located above, physically and morally, Hell, and below, in the same senses, Purgatory. In the all-important phase of mediation, Purgatory, his physical and moral motion acquires a certain logic: the past is evil; the present is a removal of the past and a lengthening of the distance from that past. The privileged present from which Dante writes what he has experienced is a metaphoric representation of what his present time will be in the future, the absence of time. Bras's space and time are equivocal, false, because they never go beyond esthetic representation. The Dantesque tripartite division is mocked here in the two metamorphoses and the vision-journey. The transformations, as we have seen, are of an esthetic nature: Brás becomes an artist and then a book. The vision reveals to him what he has always known, that the universe has no human dimension; but it reveals it in such an ironic fashion—the hippopotamus used as magical means of conveyance, for example, even more absurd than Astolfo's hippogriff—that attention is diverted from the content of the vision to the spectacle itself,

Nevertheless, we must note that human history in the vision drifts back into undifferentiated time: as far as man is concerned all centuries are the same. No change is possible, and no moral content is anywhere visible in the cosmos. Dante had something to say after his experience; Brás, very literally, has to talk about nothing. Dante had a vision, Brás has a dream, and if there is any transcendental significance in the dream, it emanates from within Brás's psyche, this scene being the only one in which a visionary, albeit a mock visionary, mode is utilized.

That the function of the dream-delirium is to make a grotesque statement about a grotesque reality may be seen by comparing it with another eschatological episode, the death of Brás's mother. Here we find no dream framework, and it would seem that we are to take the event literally: this is how Brás reacts to his mother's death. The difference between action and metaphoric representation seems to be Brás's inability to comprehend the former: "What? Was it absolutely necessary that so docile, so mild, so devout a creature, who had never caused anyone to shed a tear of grief, die in such a way, tortured, mauled by the tenacious jaws of a merciless affliction? I confess that all of it seemed dark, incongruous, insane" (p. 543/70). Brás's reaction is so "natural," his meditation on death as the end of social conventions is itself so conventional, that we are apt to forget the context in which it occurs. In effect, the scene is highly sentimental, recalling similar passages in Sterne and de Maistre, but we must recall what sort of character Brás is in order to see just what function the ruminations on death fulfill. If Brás were a novelistic character, we might expect some sort of transformation in his personality. Because he is a satiric character, however, the scene has a different value. Brás's life up until that moment had been a series of egoistic, selfish actions: his childhood greed and cruelty, his ambition to "own" a beautiful courtesan (Marcela), his scapegrace student life, and his adventures on the grand tour. Now the mirror is held up to his face: in his mother's death he sees his own. But does this change him? Only to the extent that he is now incapable of dedicating himself body and soul to any vital project since he knows where it will end. It is a moment comparable to Lazarillo's (or any *pícaro's*) "enlightenment," or the moment of *desengaño* in a Baroque text: the veil of ignorance is torn away and reality presents itself as a mirror. Brás is now ready to become a wounded soul, incapable of taking direct action, incapable of acting on his own desires, wishing for fame and glory but unable to seize them. He is now himself, sick with the incurable malady of nihilism combined with an egoistic incapacity to place himself in any social context.

What seems difficult to grasp is why Machado chose to repeat the same message. It is true that the dream is more applicable to history itself, that an event like the death of Brás's mother provides a cause, an explanation for the narrator's later relationships. It is almost as if the two events were the opening and closing of a life composed of reiterations, of a life which could "go" nowhere. What Brás may have understood, what the reader may also have understood, as a "personal tragedy" is revealed in the text to have been nothing more than the common fate of all men. Brás must be thought of as a kind of Everyman, but with this difference: he exists in a world devoid of metaphysical possibilities where salvation in the Christian sense is impossible. This transforms him into an abstraction camouflaged with personality, a name only, totally devoid of reality. And it is this abstract quality which links him with the character-types of traditional satire instead of making him a novelistic "person."

This same generalized status is manifest in all of the characters in Brás's narration. Abstraction and repetition are the hallmark of the *Memórias Póstumas*. We should remember that Brás is an author "for whom the graveyard was a cradle" (p. 511/19), that beginnings and ends in his life are peculiarly affinal. In chapter 51, Brás pronounces his "law of the equivalence of windows" (repeated in chapter 105), which for him is an ethical posture: "the way to compensate for a closed window is to open another so that one's morals can constantly ventilate one's conscience." This ironic passage may also be taken as a structural postulate: Brás cannot change or develop after his mother's death; his life consists of a number of repetitions. The people around him are really permutations of his own personality, all versions of himself.

That birth and death, creation and destruction, and many other traditionally opposed terms are actually opposite faces of the same process is a commonplace of metaphysical speculation. It is a commonplace taken ironically throughout Machado's work. The very title of his earliest long narrative, *Ressurreição* [Resurrection] (1872), points to the hero's inability to be truly reborn, and it is this persistence of character which marks all of Machado's protagonists. In the *Memórias Póstumas* the rebirth is, again, esthetic, and there is no possibility of transcending that category. Brás can never be a part of life because he was always dead. His world too is devoid of real life, locked in a permanent state of flux. Only a few social roles possess a rudimentary sort of identity: people are rich or poor, slaves, beggars, or priests. All are narcissistic; all are either victims or oppressors; and, most importantly, because of this, all are mad.

That the characters are all mad is consistent with the generic identity of the text. There may be a statement about Machado's attitude toward Brazil in this reduction of character to type, and the name of the protagonist here certainly invites an identification of him with the country in which he lives. This may further suggest that the text is in fact a true-to-life representation of life in Brazil in the nineteenth century. All of this is possible; however, it seems more useful, especially after considering the *Memórias Póstumas* in the context of Machado's other satires, where character is reduced to stereotype and society is reduced to a cardboard stageset, to think of Machado as a writer who could produce only satires.

The final cause for this sort of literary output as opposed, say, to the writing of novels may be social in that Machado's act of *mimesis* may actually be accurate for a society devoid of those elements necessary for writing novels (a specific sense of history for example). And if it is so, then one would have to say that the same kind of society is still in existence in Latin America and that the same kind of relationship that exists between Machado's texts and his world exists between the other texts examined here and their worlds. Be that as it may, it may be concluded that the novel as a genre has never manifested itself in Latin America, where writers of narrative have turned either to satire or to romance. A confirmation of this theory, a confirmation based, to be sure, on repetition, may be found in another text by Machado de Assis, *Dom Casmurro*.

2

Machado de Assis
Narrating & Lying

Dom Casmurro (1899) reiterates the techniques Machado utilizes in the *Memórias Póstumas*. Despite superficial differences, the texts are permutations of the same literary device, the fictional autobiography. Both narrators, Brás and Bento, control the point of view, Brás because he writes from beyond the grave, and Bento because he writes from beyond the graves of those whose lives are most intimately intertwined with his own. The two beguile because they lack competition, although their rhetoric ultimately shows flaws when it is seen not as the rhetoric of a character but the rhetoric of the entire text. We cannot know if the character is lying or telling the truth, and we are not concerned about this except as an indication of the text's own status in the world as a fiction. Brás and Bento are only words on a page, but they are words that invite interpretation: the ultimate thrust of their rhetoric may be said to be to seduce us in order to frustrate us. "Truths," "ideas," and "values" are all subordinated by Machado to the fiction itself.

Both Brás and Bento underscore their identity as books by discussing their methodology: Brás begins his "history" with his death; Bento explains the title, the words that stand as a threshold to his discourse, before he gives his reasons for writing. Like all writers of autobiography, the two have something to teach: Brás exposes the meaninglessness of his life (and, it would seem, all lives), and Bento the perfidy of human kind. Bento's text is a verbal reconstruction of his past, an enterprise he had attempted on a physical level by building a replica of his childhood home. When duplication failed, he turned to metaphor, that is, to language. Again, what the actions of a character like Bento reveal is not intended to give the reader insight into the inner workings of a mind, but to present a particular syndrome as a literary text. This syndrome is not to be associated with an individual but with a type: Bento and Brás are not people but stereotypes; their texts are not histories but moral or psychological satires.

One major difference between Brás and Bento is the openness of the first and the closed quality of the second. Memoirs, what Brás writes, are not confessions, although both involve considerable self-explanation and self-justification. Brás does not unburden himself by revealing something; in fact, he makes his reader as uncomfortable as he is by his desperate statements. Bento writes in order to recover his past, he says, and it is his narrative, the entire text, which most nearly approximates a confession. He confesses in the way a criminal in a detective novel confesses, by dropping clues, not as someone who is intentionally baring his soul to the world. The latter wants to be seen as an example, the former simply wants to be caught.

When Rousseau actually confesses a crime in his *Confessions*, we are not surprised in the slightest. In the scene in which he reviles himself for having caused a girl to run afoul of the law, he says:

> Nevertheless I have never been able to bring myself to relieve my heart by revealing this in private to a friend. Not with the most intimate friend, not even with Mme de Warens, has this been possible. The most that I could do was to confess that I had a terrible deed on my conscience, but I have never said in what it consisted. The burden, therefore, has rested till this day on my conscience without any relief; and I can affirm that the desire to some extent to rid myself of it has greatly contributed to my resolution of writing these *Confessions*. [1]

The peculiar aspect of these confessions is that Rousseau, a man, telling us the story of his life, transforms himself into a character simply by committing his words to the page. The reverse phenomenon, and here is the source of their irony, occurs in texts like the *Memórias Póstumas* and *Dom Casmurro*. That a man is capable of any sort of action is perfectly natural, but that a fiction should present a figure capable not only of confessing, of sinning, but also of lying, makes us see not a higher level of verisimilitude, but the "fictitious" quality of any text. There is no truth in words, just a semblance of it; behind the words there is nothing. Through the bizarre alchemy of the printed word Rousseau, Brás, and Bento become identical quantities: there is no absolute demarcation of truth and lie in any of their texts.

And yet it is possible to talk about Bento's aims in writing his text, even if what he produces is the result of a kind of madnesss, jealousy. Machado does not merely present a jealous character in Bento, but a character who *is* jealousy. That is, Bento's wound, like Brás's incapacity to act after his mother's death, is his inability to possess anything completely. Possession in this case is not ownership but the ability to see people and objects as forming part of one's intimate domain. No matter what he does, Bento will always have his possessions usurped, even if he must himself invent the usurper. This is the way in which his madness works: he, a new version of Tantalus, is in a situation in which both past and future flee from him. He dwells in a present he renders horrible by interpreting it from the perspective of his jealousy.

Machado creates for Bento, as he does not for Brás, a psychological causality that recalls the biological inheritance theory of Zola, even if this comparison would have annoyed the Brazilian writer. There is no father figure in Bento's youth because his father dies during his childhood; only his portrait remains, in fact two portraits, one literal and one metaphorical. The literal portrait hangs in the replica-house Bento has constructed, and is painted in such a way that his father's round eyes "accompany me everywhere, an effect of the composition that frightened me when I was a child" (p. 814/16).[2] This portrait is referred to again later in the same passage, and Bento imagines that the portrait of his mother, hanging next to his father's, is saying, "I am completely yours, my handsome knight!" To which he imagines his father to be saying, "Look, all of you, at how much this girl loves me" (p. 815/16). That his mother is looking at his father and his father at him is a detail he makes much of, and it is his being excluded from the mother-to-father circuit which marks, in primitive psychological terms, his "problem." His mother is in one way entirely devoted to his father, even if at the same time she is a perfect mother. Her permanent mourning, her having vowed to make her son a priest, her overly protective nature (which deforms Bento's boyhood) all contribute to Bento's being close to the object of his desires, his mother, without having any opportunity to resolve his dilemma.

His father is dead; therefore there can be no competing with him. He is in fact like God, invisible but ubiquitous and omnipotent. He cannot be killed or usurped at any level, and this stifling of Bento's oedipal energies further deforms his development, rendering him curiously impotent. It is as though Cain were in the Garden with Abel, Eve, and his own wife: Bento cannot punish his mother for being unfaithful to him (because she is faithful to her husband), so he creates a surrogate mother in his own wife, Capitú. (That he and Capitú fall in love in the family garden reinforces the biblical resonance of the entire text.) Bento cannot destroy his father, but he can destroy a surrogate father by turning his best friend, Escobar, into Capitú's lover and the father of his own son Ezequiel. With Escobar dead, figuratively killed by Bento, although he actually drowns, Bento may further punish his parents by symbolically killing his only potential rival, his own son, whom he redefines as illegitimate. With the son and Capitú dead, the possibility of time's altering his situation is eliminated: Bento, like Cronus, is absolutely secure because he cannot be in any way challenged by real or imaginary rivals. The text closes the circle of time completely: it ends with Ezequiel's death, the moment Bento can begin to write. With all dead, Bento can transform them into characters. The text is his swan-song, his own elegy, since he too must "die" in order to become his own subject.

Naturally this dying is a kind of death-in-life. Reduced to lifelessness by the production of this fictitious self-history and justification—his real bastard child—Bento has literally nowhere to go. He states that he will now begin to write a historical work, the *História dos Subúrbios* to which he refers at the outset of his discourse. He was distracted from that task by the paintings of the sculpted busts of Nero, Augustus, Masinissa, and Caesar which "said" to him that "since they hadn't enabled me to reconstruct times past, I should take up my pen and tell about a few" (p. 808/6). What archeological reconstruction fails to do, fiction can, at some expense, accomplish. Bento will become his own father, in the same metaphorical fashion in which he is seen by his mother to be the very image of his father (in chapter 99), by engendering his own self-portrait.

It is fitting the painted busts on the wall should incite Bento to write his own portrait, especially so if we consider the character of those depicted. Three are Roman emperors, and one, Masinissa, is a North African king allied with the Romans against Carthage. A cursory examination of the biographies of the four reveals a host of aberrations: Masinissa, one of the greatest North African figures of antiquity, sent his wife, Sophonisba (who had been the wife of a rival—and who is the subject of a tragedy by Trissino), poison after the Romans expressed displeasure at the union. "Grande César," as Bento calls him, was a sodomite, a sensualist, and rapacious. Augustus was cruel and an adulterer. Nero, the most debauched of the lot, committed incest with his mother, was a sodomite, a profligate, a matricide, and the murderer of practically all his relations.

In a hyperbolic form we see in these men a portrait of Bento. While not an overt homosexual, he is nevertheless effeminate in his ways, clinging to his mother's apron strings, incapable of telling his mother himself that he does not want to be a priest; he is in this sense exactly the opposite of Escobar, who makes his own way in the world on his own strength and merit. In chapter 67, Bento sees his mother's death as a means of escaping the seminary, although, as he says, "Filial piety failed for an instant, at the sight of complete freedom revealed by the disappearance of the debt and the debtor [he refers to his mother's vow to make him a priest]; it was only for an instant, less than an instant, the hundredth part of an instant, but even so, it was enough to complicate my affliction with remorse" (p. 877/136). This confession of a lapse in filial piety is a means of hoodwinking the reader. Certainly another mother-son relationship is evoked by the text, and referred to concretely as well in chapter 54, that of Saint Augustine and his mother, Saint Monica. Does Bento want us to see him as the sinful son who becomes a saint? No doubt he does, but the association actually succeeds in inspiring contrary thoughts.

Bento is an adulterer in thought if not in fact. Whether or not Escobar's wife, Sancha, actually flirts with him, as he states in chapter 120, cannot be determined, but we do have Bento's confession of his intentions and the curious chapter 129, in which he apostrophizes Sancha, telling her not to continue to read his discourse except at her own risk. Why all this posturing? There is something inconsistent, false, in all of Bento's references to Sancha. He rounds off his remarks to her by quoting from *Purgatory*, saying that she and he will meet again in heaven, "renewed, like new plants, *come piante novelle,/ Rinovellate di novelle fronde*" (p. 929/236). The quotation is grotesque in this context and more so when we complete the poetic sentence in which it occurs:

> Io ritornai de la santissima onda
> rifatto sí come piante novelle
> rinovellate di novelle fronda,
> puro e disposto a salire a le stelle.

Dante has just been immersed in the river Eunoè, which revives the soul's memory of the good it did on earth. In a perverse sense, the text is Bento's Eunoè because he forgets (or omits) any references to unrepented acts of evil and presents himself to the reader purified. Another word which seems important here is *onda*, the term Dante uses to refer to the river. It might also refer to the waves that drowned Escobar and allowed Bento to convert him into Capitú's lover and his own surrogate father.

Like his matricide, like his incest, and like his adultery, his murder of his wife and child never reaches the level of literal truth. He exiles Capitú to Switzerland, where she dies; and he sends his son on an archeological expedition to Jerusalem, where he dies. He confesses he wished his son would contract leprosy there, but he publishes his repentence, as he does whenever he records having evil thoughts. The means by which these deaths occur is, ultimately, irrelevant: the people die just as if his wishes had come true.

One of the supposed differences between fiction and what we

loosely call nonfiction is that in the former the *artifex* can shape events as he sees fit, while in the latter he is constrained to respect some external reality. No historian would try to turn Waterloo into a military victory for Napoleon, although interpretations of the battle's meaning might be myriad. The meaning any historical event has is determined by the "story" in which the historian situates it.[3] An event in itself can have no meaning, any more than a part of speech out of its linguistic context. Bento's history of himself is not necessarily false—from his point of view, from the perspective of jealousy—because it is not so much the events he describes but the sequence and significance he creates for them which interest us.

We see that Bento's narrative is really a metaphor for a totally different story; actual events simply represent the process by which he creates a "deeper" narrative to relieve his repressions. The creation of a surrogate family, the ritualistic murder of that metaphoric family—this is the real story beneath the self-history. Like Brás, Bento describes the way in which he came to find himself in a certain state, but unlike Brás he tells how he exploited that state. Brás becomes socially immobile after his mother's death; Bento is psychologically warped because of his father's death. The only real difference between the stories is the method by which each rationalizes or interprets his reality.

For both Brás and Bento the ritual of telling the story is a means of salvation. Brás still wants to attain the fame and glory which eluded him in life, and Bento wants to recapture the past—and vindicate himself. Each nominally tells how he came to be what he is; that is, the plot of each text is supposed to be a description of how A through process Y became B. In neither case is this model quite accurate. Both have an initial situation, A, which is of a different length in each; but it is as if that phase were not related to the process at all. When Brás is young, he does certain things, and certain characters who later reappear are introduced (the slave Prudêncio, Marcela, Quincas Borba, and Eusébia, for example), but their real importance is only attained in the second phase of the discourse, when they become aspects of Brás himself. The initial phase of Brás's life is simply an introduction, and it is only with the death of his mother that he becomes what he is meant to be. That is, there is no promise that A will become B, and consequently there is no fully organized plot. The *Memórias Póstumas* are based on repetition, not process, and in this they differ from typical picaresque narratives, which depend on accumulation, a heaping-up of episodes, although even here the episodes soon seem to be permutations of each other.

Bento's initial phase is dramatically short because he can only remember the period before his father's death in the vaguest ways. He is what he is meant to be from the beginning of the narrative. This exploitation of a state in both the *Memórias Póstumas* and *Dom Casmurro* is a strategy intended to run counter to the kind of narrative that emulates linear history. Naturally, there can be no narrative without linearity, but a narrative meant to lead back to its beginnings, which eschews the description of a world of objects for the repetition of one metaphor in diverse forms is clearly setting its sights on targets alien to literary realism. These targets might more easily be found in the poetry of the second half of the nineteenth century, the symbolist exploration and representation of a mood or a sensation, and it is in this context that we turn to Jorge Luis Borges and Adolfo Bioy Casares, who postulate and enact an esthetics of narrative based on metaphor.

Adolfo Bioy Casares
Satire & Self-portrait

In a perverse, sardonic essay of 1932, "Narrative Art and Magic,"[1] Jorge Luis Borges talks about causality in the novel. Naturally, there are few people who would call William Morris's *The Life and Death of Jason* or Edgar Allan Poe's *Narrative of A. Gordon Pym* novels, but these are nevertheless the texts Borges uses as examples. The selection constitutes some sort of esthetic evaluation of the novel as a genre, an ambiguous but a far from positive one. At the end of the essay, Borges recapitulates his main points: "I have delineated two causal processes: the natural, which is the incessant result of uncontrollable and infinite operations; the magic, which is lucid and limited, and where details prophesy. In the novel I think the only honorable choice lies with the second. Let the first remain for psychological simulation" (p. 91). While Borges's concept of what a novel might be is, to say the least, mysterious, his ideas of what should and should not be done in narrative literature are clear. The events in a novelistic plot cannot be the haphazard flow of everyday life, but must be artificial, held together by contextual affinities or by actual similarities. There must be some sort of link between events, otherwise there would be an undifferentiated rush of events in the discourse, what Borges later calls "the Asiatic disorder of the real world" (p. 90). Following what Borges says in the essay, we see that he is not sympathetic to the novel— whatever he thinks the novel is—and attempts to point out that the only "honorable" solution to the problem of narrating is the establishment of some sort of unity within the text itself.

This rage for order is presented rather vaguely here, but it is stated with much greater precision, about as much as Borges can muster, in his prologue to Adolfo Bioy Casares's *La invención de Morel* (1940).[2] Like all of Borges's essays, this prologue blends the brilliant with the outrageous (which for Borges is "common sense"), but it should be noted that it is imbued with two of his well-known prejudices: the tendency present in his thought and work, since his flirtation with *Ultraísmo*, to see metaphor as the nucleus of literature—similar to the imagism of Pound and Eliot—and his intense dislike of the novel, or any extended form which requires explanatory or transitional passages. This displeasure may be an extension of the kind of taste Valéry exhibited in a remark quoted by Breton, the famous refusal to write "La marquise sortit à cinq heures":

> By contrast, the realistic attitude, inspired by positivism, from Saint Thomas Aquinas to Anatole France, clearly seems to me to be hostile to any intellectual or moral advancement . . . . An amusing result of this state of affairs, in literature for example, is the generous supply of novels. Each person adds his personal little "observation" to the whole. As a cleansing antidote to all this, M. Paul Valéry recently suggested that an anthology be compiled in which the largest possible number of opening passages from novels be offered . . . . Such a thought reflects great credit on Paul Valéry who, some time ago, speaking of novels, assured me that, so far as he was concerned, he would continue to refrain from writing: "The Marquise went out at five."[3]

The importance of this quotation, not only in this context but also because its ideas are relevant to Julio Cortázar[4] and other writers under scrutiny, justifes its presence. It is curious to find both Breton and Borges inveighing against literary realism, but it would seem to be an aspect of the avant-garde of the twenties and thirties, a reaction against the verisimilitude of the nineteenth century. In the case of Borges it may also represent a Crocean reaction against Hegelian historiography, although such a proposition is difficult to prove. There is, of course, more than historical circumstance behind the negation. There is a desire to turn literature away from the representational toward the metaphoric. It may be that this corresponds to the disintegration of bourgeois belief in the notion of material progress; it may also mark a turning away from the idea that history is the product of the dialectical process of struggle and synthesis. But the historical process has never seemed immanent in Latin America; that is, as a colonial culture, Latin America has always seen itself on the verge of a historical process instead of having one already within its fiber. The turn away from realism as a doctrine, an action observable in Zola's works, marks the coming together of colonies and metropolis in certain aspects of their world-view, if not in their economic relationships.

In his prologue to *Morel*, Borges continues his polemic against the novel and literary realism, training his sights this time on another critic, José Ortega y Gasset, and his essay "The Dehumanization of Art" (1925). Borges begins by ironically attacking Ortega's historicism, especially his belief that "it's difficult to imagine the formulation of an adventure capable of interesting our superior sensibility."[5] This belief that Western sensibility had evolved or matured to such an extent that it could no longer tolerate adventure literature, and that the only kind of literature possible was to be psychological in nature obviously grated on Borges's own sensibility. He begins his attack by noting that the "novela de peripecias," or adventure novel, is "an artificial object which suffers no unjustified part" (p. 12/6), while the "realist" and "psychological" novel (identical for Borges) attempts to be a copy of life. The result of this attempt to create texts that make us forget their "being verbal artifice" (p. 12/6) is a failure of art, the production of formless verbal floods that negate the basic principle of all art: artificiality. The imposition of a rigorous, Aristotelian cause-and-effect plot on a story elevates it, in Borges's eyes, above the realist, psychological novel. Our age, he asserts, with its detective novels, with texts like James's *The Turn of the Screw* or Kafka's *Der Prozess*, is expert in this kind of plot-making. It would seem that Borges understands the "novela de peripecias" to include what we would call romance and satire, although it is clear that Borges has no great interest in genre theory or, for that matter, in terminological clarity.

As we shall see when we deal with *Rayuela*, Cortázar felt he was identifying a crisis in modern literature when he had his fictitious author Morelli attack the "traditional novel," but it is clear that the psychological, realist novel had been on the wane since Flaubert.[6] The moment novelists gave up their claims to be historians, the moment character ceased to be linked to history and began to exist as an excuse for itself, the orthodox novel no longer held hegemony among the other classes of extended narrative. While it is true that an author like Faulkner could revive it in *Sartoris*, the "novel" in the second half of the nineteenth century was tending toward either satire or romance. Such dissimilar writers as Melville, George Eliot, Zola, and Machado de Assis do have one thing in common: they reduce society's role in their works to that of setting; they explore character either as a social phenomenon or as the result of a given set of circumstances, such as biological inheritance or property tenure.

Bioy Casares in *Morel* creates a series of linked metaphors to describe the transformation of a man into an artist and, finally, the artist into art. Like Machado, Bioy uses the first-person narrator, but unlike the Brazilian, he delineates more sharply the "textual" nature of his work by defining it as a diary. What we are reading is a remainder, a leftover, and by emphasizing this dead or inert side of any work of art, its existence as the object of attention, Bioy declares its alien nature. The reader can never have direct contact with the narrator: he is not speaking to us or confessing his sins to God in our presence. Like Sartre's *La Nausée*, *Morel* is itself a kind of cadaver. The "new" Roquentin exists beyond the text (and the life) he has left behind, and, in the same way, we are encouraged to follow his example. Bioy has no overt ideological message in his text; there is no hortatory aspect to his satire; and yet, it is clear that he is making an esthetic statement. He is interested in expressing what it is that the artist becomes when he commits himself to his work.

To demonstrate his point, Bioy revitalizes the story of the man who goes to a desert island. Borges himself notes that H. G. Wells's *The Island of Dr. Moreau* is alluded to in Bioy's title; we might add that such a reference would automatically conjure up Swift, Defoe, Stevenson (also mentioned by Borges), Verne, Dante, and a host of others. One island text suggests another because they all deal with extraordinary circumstances, a hiatus in "normal" affairs. Even true stories about island visits contain the element of adventure that stimulates our appetite for the exotic, which, even when real, is somehow beyond literary realism. No matter what the text is, the sea we cross divides us from the world of our dreams. The sea may be real, but it is also our subconscious; and for that reason, no voyage to an island can be absolutely free from symbolic or metaphoric traits. Ordinary tourist advertising realized this long ago and continues to play on our desire for adventure.

Bioy's story is simple. A man fleeing from political persecution seeks refuge on an island supposed to be the epicenter of a fatal disease. Once on the island he begins to notice strange things: the seasons seem to accelerate, and then, with no warning, people appear out of nowhere. He writes to leave testimony about the climatic change, but his diary changes as he grows increasingly interested in the strange visitors. This interest becomes critical when he falls in love with Faustine, one of the women in the company. He learns that to them he is invisible, although he only learns why when he discovers that they are not really people but images projected by cameras operated by the tides. They have bulk, need no screen, and will last as long as the machines function. Desperate, the unnamed diarist decides to interpolate himself into the film (an act which kills all who are photographed) so that anyone who comes to the island will think he is part of the original.

The protagonist's life consists of a series of spatial reductions. First he shares a political and social life with others, then he becomes a fugitive, constantly in motion. On the island his possibilities for movement are limited. He has fled society and history; all he has left is his own mind, the island, and the various texts he projects and the diary he writes. The withdrawal from the world (for no matter what reason) is a metaphor for the writer who withdraws from the world to compose his text. The voyage to the island is that withdrawal, just as the blank page is the island which will be "populated" by words.

The reader, again the writer's mirror twin, recapitulates the writer's self-exile when he withdraws from the world to read the text, which is his island. The portrait of Saint Ambrose that

Augustine gives in the *Confessions* (book 6, chapter 3) constitutes
a perfect image of this act: Augustine describes the saint reading
silently, so absorbed in his reading that he does not notice the
presence of other people in the room. The reader, like the narrator, is alone on an island filled with people.

Our relationship with the text is as complex as that of the
narrator with the images he finds on the island. He cannot rec-
oncile himself to the idea that they are not real (his last words
are a plea for someone to make Faustine truly aware of his
existence) just as we might be tempted to affix a personality and
a psychology to the narrator himself. We must realize that such
an act would betray both the text and our roles as readers. The
lesson Bioy implants in his text is the concept of art as suicide,
an act mirrored in the suicide the unwitting reader commits
when he takes fictions for realities: to create a text means to
create an artist, and to do that it is necessary to "kill" a man.
Morel is elegiac in that it celebrates the death of a man who has
achieved immortality, the ironic immortality of art which requires the death of a man. Like "Borges and I," although less
ironic because it is not toying with the idea of autobiography,
the mode whereby the self is immortalized by being transformed
into a fiction, *Morel* is concerned with the distinctions between
the artist as man and man as artist. It is no less involved with our
identities as individuals and our identities as readers. We must
also give up something, "die" a bit, before we are reborn in the
act of interpretation, the act by which we liberate ourselves from
the text, deforming it into our own image. A failure to interpret
is the situation described in Borges's "Tlön, Uqbar, Orbis Tertius,"[7] where all fictions are subsumed into the insidious and
false encyclopedia because no one treats the fiction as a fiction.

Both Machado's and Bioy's texts invite interpretation, but
they also demand one sort of interpretation instead of another.
The fact that the "real" narrator is always separated from us by a
linguistic void is never attenuated in these books by the creation
of sentimental links between us and him. We are made to realize
that what is speaking to us is a text and not a person, that if
there ever was a person behind these words he is irretrievably
lost. The narratives themselves are metaphors for communication, since they are composed without the presence of any

known listeners, again in direct contrast to Augustine's ideal
listener or the gentleman who asked Lazarillo to write his
autobiography. It is the nature of first person narratives always
to be "about" something, even if that subject is forever absent,
replaced by words, that is, by metaphors. This is less explicit,
perhaps, in Machado than in Bioy, who resuscitates the Renaissance found-and-edited manuscript to underline further his
speaker's purely verbal identity.

In *Morel*, the verbal artifact is ironically juxtaposed to another
absence, Morel's film. The film literally swallows up the narrator, who can look at himself in it in the same way someone
who has written his autobiography can read about himself.
There is of course a difference: the narrator has deliberately
inserted himself in someone else's creation, hoping that his in-
trusion will pass unnoticed by newcomers. In any case, the
elegiac note is again sounded, and the dying man sees himself
transformed into a work of art, although that work of art is itself
bizarre. Morel, not an artist but a sentimental scientist, creates a
tranche de vie, a direct copy of life. In explaining to his friends
what he has done, he states: "My abuse consists in having
photographed you without permission. Of course mine is not a
common photographic method; it is my latest invention. We
shall live in that photograph forever. Imagine a stage on which
our life during these last seven days will be acted out completely" (p. 99/58). The machine neither edits nor selects; it simply captures whatever images it can. It is the narrator who imposes his will on the film when he creates a new reality by
interpolating himself. He does what the reader should not: he
enters a world with which he can have no real contact.

Paradoxically, however, the text, like the film, requires the
reader to "make something" of it. Why should this invitation to
interpret be part of the text instead of part of the reader? How do
we know *Morel* is a metaphorical text? There is no answer except
to point out the elements of the text itself: the island voyage, the
decision to write, the relationship between the narrator and the
woman in the film (a variation of the Romantic *belle dame sans
merci* theme, where she comes to stand for the text itself in its
complete otherness), and, of course, Borges's preface, which
prejudices the reader. These same elements may nevertheless re-

main insignificant to another reader. Unlike Renaissance literature, where mythology, symbolic names, and rhyme signalled
to the reader what sort of reading he was to do, these texts leave
everything to the reader's instincts. Perhaps the examination of
another text by Bioy Casares, *Plan de evasión* (1945), may help to
establish some of the landmarks in this perpetually shifting
metaphoric literature.

4

Adolfo Bioy Casares
The Lying Compass

Bioy's *Plan de evasión* (1945) is more clearly a case of metaphoric writing, of satire, than *Morel*. *Morel* is deliberately nonallusive, except for its title and one or two other incidental references to painters or authors; but *Plan* is shot through with literary allusions and references to cultural matters in general. It is as though Bioy were attempting to tantalize the reader into drawing connections between his and other texts which would ultimately prove either misleading or useless. This technique recalls Borges, whose myriad references are a plague to all his readers; and both authors may have the same goal in mind: to proffer the expectation of meaning to the reader and withdraw it before it can ever become a reality.

Bioy creates metaphorical texts, but he carefully leaves open the concept of referent. The text becomes something like a historical event (see above, p. 27) in that it can have any number of meanings depending on the context into which it is inserted. Indeed, this simultaneous inscrutability and *disponibilité* underlines the close relationship between all kinds of extended narratives and the writing of chronicles. Critics like Lukács,[1] who for reasons of symmetry want the novel (and, we assume, other narrative forms) to be the counterpart in the bourgeois era of the epic in an earlier age, destroy the value of genre study. The idea that the novel is our epic is much too "neat" to be accurate, especially because it fulfills the critic's idealized view of modern history and not the actual state of esthetic affairs. Texts like those of Machado, Bioy, or Cabrera Infante (see chap. 7) do not strive (and fail) to be totalities; they are deliberately incomplete, encouraging the reader to participate to the fullest in the creative process, at no small risk to both parties. We know *Plan* is "about" something, but we will never know what.

Plan is, ostensibly, the prejudiced presentation of the letters of Enrique Nevers, who had been sent to Cayenne in 1913 by his hostile uncle, Antoine Brissac. The uncle's goal seems to be either to condemn Nevers or, to say the least, discredit him. In this the uncle is not unlike Bento in *Dom Casmurro* when he speaks about his wife, but in this text the uncle is an actor only in the sense that it is he who presents the letters to the reader. This is a grotesque elaboration of the "editor" device used in *Morel* and would seem to be a reminiscence of the complicated mass of editing and translating involved in *Don Quijote*. In fact, the very drama of the text, Nevers's discovery that the warden of the penal colony on Devil's Island has been altering the perception of his inmates so they will think they are living on individual island paradises, is virtually "lost" in the editorial fluctuations.

The text's form mirrors its basic principle: what we see is not what is but what our senses and our brain tell us we see. Again, the esthetic ramifications of such hypotheses are myriad. They transcend the Renaissance topic of appearance and reality precisely because they suggest that appearance is reality. The only possible *desengaño* in a situation like this is to realize that there is no message, no secret hidden under the surface of things, that the surface is all. But even this cannot halt the process of interpretation, which does not pretend to alter the text's meaning so much as to situate it in contexts where other possibilities are affixed to it.

The idea of the island explored so intensely in *Morel* is restated here: what the warden, Castel, does for his prisoners, who are already on an island, is to create for them another island; he does this in a spirit of charity, science working for the benefit of man. Naturally, what he creates are monsters, creatures whose "dérèglement de tous les sens" is a physical truth. The irony of Rimbaud's desideratum in this context, the irony of a synesthesia more absolute than any ever dreamed of by either the

symbolists or I. A. Richards, is that it is not achieved through
words but through surgery—at least in the most literal reading
of the text. But what happens here, as in *Morel*, demands interpretation. To come to any island is to leave the world behind;
it is a transfer from the macro- to the microcosm, from the public
world of the conscious, the world with which the ego interacts,
to the private world of the subconscious, comparable to the world
in which, in Freudian terms, the ego interacts with the id and
the superego.

If we establish equivalences, if we see the text as an island, the
writer's as he composes it and the reader's as he deciphers it,
then other possibilities materialize. In *Morel* the narrator undergoes a metamorphosis and, like Proteus, becomes an immortal.
If metamorphosis is the ruling idea, the dominant metaphor in
Morel, we may say that derangement is the guiding principle in
Plan, particularly literary derangement. If *Morel* is "about" how
a man becomes an artist and how another man becomes a
reader, *Plan* is concerned with the effects on the public of its
encounter with a work of art. In this sense, it may be seen as an
extrapolation of the encounter the narrator of *Morel* has with the
images: until he finds out what they really are, he thinks he is
mad. This is exactly what the reader of *Plan* experiences; he
knows that the uncle-editor is biased and that the text is
therefore twisted to conform with his understanding of his
nephew's sins; but just what it is that lies behind the nephew's
letters, his relationship with certain family papers, with a girl
(Irene), with his cousin Xavier is left deliberately ambiguous. All
we know is that Enrique Nevers is either guilty or innocent of a
certain crime (we never learn what it is), is either loved or not by
Irene, is either mad or sane, and is either dead or alive by the
end of the narrative. Such an abundance of clarity is likely to
dazzle almost any reader.

This is the point. The text is a series of dead ends, both in its
plot and in its allusions. All of the elements seem to be relevant
to the story as a totality, but that totality never emerges. This
discord between the whole and its parts may be exemplified by
the references to Rimbaud which appear throughout the text.
Early in the book the narrator-uncle reports, "Those days
[Nevers] spent in the capital of the penal colony seemed to him *a*

season in hell" (pp. 11–12/3),[2] to which an indulgent editor adds
a gratuitous footnote, "une saison en enfer." A little later the
narrator refers to two ships, "one Sunday the Schelcher, the
next the Rimbaud" (p. 17/7). Then, much later, Nevers reads in
notes left by Castel, *"A noir, E blanc, I rouge* ... is not an absurd
affirmation; it is an improvised answer" (p. 154/106). There may
be more references or allusions, and some of the above are repeated, but these are the most obvious.

But what is the relationship between Rimbaud and *Plan*? To
call a stay in a disagreeable place "une saison en enfer" is to be
pedantic and trite, so we may conclude that the reference is not
intended to impress us, especially with the addition of the
French original in a footnote. Perhaps its only purpose is to
introduce Rimbaud as a type, the "poète maudit," and to make
the reader think about his techniques. This second idea is
somewhat tenuous, especially if we recall that in *Une saison en
enfer* Rimbaud refutes the association of vowels and colors he
makes in the earlier "Voyelles," from *Poésies*:

> J'inventai la couleur des voyelles!—*A* noir, *E* blanc, *I* rouge, *O*
> bleu, *U* vert.—Je réglai la forme et le mouvement de chaque
> consonne, et, avec des rhythmes instinctifs, je me flattai d'in-
> venter un verbe poétique accessible, un jour ou l'autre, à tous
> les sens.[3]

This ironic passage might lead us back to the "Voyelles," but
there too we are ultimately baffled. As Castel's reference to the
poem suggests, it is not Rimbaud, as stylist or as "poète
maudit," who is at stake but the concept of sensation or the
mind's organization and interpretation of sensation. It does not
seem terribly important for an understanding of *Plan* to link the
ship Rimbaud to Rimbaud's "Bateau ivre," although one must
wonder why Bioy insists on referring to the French poet. It may
be because Enrique Nevers is himself a poet, but again, this is
certainly a circuitous association. It depends on the reader's rec-
ognition of some link between Nevers and Rimbaud, of the allusions to Rimbaud, and the reader's ability to connect only one
aspect (synesthesia, let us say) of Rimbaud's verse with the matters dealt with in *Plan*.

This unnecessary complication is characteristic of all external references in *Plan* and seems to say to the reader that he will never be able to trace the text back to its origins, whatever they are. Naturally, even its consistency in this is inconsistent. In one of the rare conversations between Nevers and Castel, it is revealed that Nevers is reading Plutarch's essay on Isis and Osiris. When Castel reproaches him for wasting time on such antiquated trash, Nevers replies, "I'm interested in this book. It deals with symbols" (p. 51/32). The book not only deals with symbols but also investigates the differences between proper and improper readings of myths; in short, it deals with problems of interpretation. It is this sort of allusion which sheds light on *Plan*, not the references to Rimbaud or to nineteenth-century investigators of hypnotism or to Goethe's book on colors. Allusions such as the one to Plutarch or scenes like the one in which it is revealed that the character Dreyfus is called Dreyfus because of his admiration for the historical Dreyfus and for no other reason, clear matters up to some extent. From these we learn that what is happening may not be important in itself, but may refer to something important: the name Dreyfus is a symbol; the man who bears it is unimportant. This same character idealizes Zola, because Zola defended the real Dreyfus, and Victor Hugo, because his name sounds like the name of an early governor of the colony, Victor Hugues. (This name is doubly confusing for this reader since Victor Hugues is a character in a work by Alejo Carpentier, *El siglo de las luces*.) That is, the associations made within the text, as well as the associations the reader makes by himself, are all material which contributes in one way or another to a reading of the text; they are designed to vitiate the concept of the "correct" reading.

Interpretation here is a kind of "guilt by association." If something sounds like something else, Hugo-Hugues, or if it is connected with something else by means of repetition, Dreyfus-Dreyfus, the reader is tempted to make something of the association. The pitfall in the creation or deciphering of metaphors is to assume that they do in fact have a single, discoverable meaning, and it is on this misconception Bioy Casares pounces. When the text says, "On the dock, waiting for me, was a dark Jew, a certain Dreyfus" (p. 18/7), we automatically associate him with the real Dreyfus, who was alive at the time of the narrative

(1913). Bioy depends on our association of the two names with the same man, and he does it in order to frustrate our expectations.

This invitation to misread is referred to in the text by the word *camouflage*. When Nevers scrutinizes Devil's Island carefully, he discovers "the ominous truth," it is camouflaged. This leads him to a series of conjectures until at the end of the book it is explained that the buildings, in which the men operated on by Castel are housed, are painted (inside and out) in such a way that they look to a normal person as if they are camouflaged. The men within see a seascape and tropical islands instead of patches of color. But what is most important is the complete absence of anything beneath that surface: there is nothing "hidden" in this text, just as Castel camouflaged nothing when he painted the walls.

Those who read *Plan* thinking it a rite of passage are sadly disillusioned when they finish. All seems resolved in the experiments with sensation; at least, almost all. The problem of the fate of the protagonist is left unresolved; he vanishes. The text too will vanish after the reader finishes reading the last word, the last piece of a letter compiled by the fictitious uncle-editor. What he has just experienced is nothing more or less than a confrontation with a totally metaphoric text whose subject is metaphor. Everything in *Plan* stands for something else, but just what that something is is never explained. It is not important that it is left a mystery because this is just what is supposed to happen. How better to explore the nature of metaphor than to create a colossal metaphor? The symbolist strategy of the re-created sensation or premeditated effect is an obvious ploy here (another gesture toward Rimbaud perhaps), except that this is an entirely cerebral situation, one linked with words and words alone.

Bioy Casares's metaphoric representation of the artist and art in self-reflecting fictions was certainly unique in the context of Latin American literature in the 1940s, and the abstruseness of the texts may account for the dearth of critical material on them. Authors who investigate many of the same problems, Julio Cortázar and Severo Sarduy, who are both part of the "Boom" of the 60s, have received much more attention. Cortázar's principal inquiry into the complex relationship between artist and text, *Rayuela,* is much more mechanical in its approach to the problem. Cortázar himself seems much more concerned with constructing dialogues or monologues in which ideas about literature are expressed than in presenting his thoughts in a completely metaphoric fashion. This makes him seem a much more timid experimenter than Bioy, despite the fact that *Rayuela* proposes to attack traditional forms of literary discourse by disordering reading sequence.

The parallels between the works of Severo Sarduy and those of Bioy are striking in spite of the fact that Sarduy and Bioy have radically different intellectual formations. If Bioy's roots lead back to Borges's notion of narrative as he expresses it in "Narrative Art and Magic" and in the preface to *Morel,* Sarduy's may be traced through the pages of *Tel Quel,* Roland Barthes, Lévi-Strauss, Heidegger, and, ultimately, Jakobson and Saussure. It is a bizarre coincidence that Jakobson's adaptation of Saussure, his association of diachrony with narrative realism, and synchrony with poetic metaphor, should be a parallel to Borges's adaptation of Frazer's two kinds of magic (mentioned by Jakobson), magic worked through contiguity and magic worked through analogy. Borges's invectives against literary realism in favor of metaphoric writing, and Jakobson's objective observation of the differences between these modes of writing are also fortuitously parallel. The result in both cases was the composition, by Bioy and Sarduy, of texts which are highly metaphorical, texts which are in fact metaphors. It is true that Sarduy does not use Bioy's island-and-invention schema, and he departs even more radically from Bioy's superficially comprehensible narratives (they might be taken for science fiction), but the texts are nevertheless similar: they are works that can only be understood as metaphors on metaphor, metaliterary texts designed to show what literature is.

5

Severo Sarduy/
Vital Signs

Severo Sarduy's *De donde son los cantantes* (1965) may be said to
constitute an allegory of language, or more specifically, of the
language of Cuba. We should understand allegory in this context not so much as a kind of literature but as a way of reading
literature. In the ancient world, in Quintilian for example, allegory is a situation in which a meaning exactly opposite to the
meaning of the words is intended or one in which words say one
thing and mean another. For Sarduy, as for Derrida, words are
arbitrarily chosen signs, and printed words doubly arbitrary,
doubly metaphoric signs, marks that stand for linguistic signs
which stand in turn for something else. Any conjugation of
these written signs therefore constitutes a case of allegorical activity, since we know that we are at least twice removed from
anything like reality when we deal with the written word. We
know, further, that the context in which these written signs
appear, a literary text, is one in which nothing is communicated
directly. What Sarduy's rhetoric aims at is a literal reading of the
text—but this of course is a pun.

Theologians have for centuries been accustomed to see the
Bible as a text in which more than one level of meaning is
present. These levels, in Aquinas and, ultimately, in Dante,
were codified into four levels: the literal, the allegorical, the
tropological, and the anagogical. The literal has two or three
separate modes of existence: the words are composed of letters
and must therefore have an individual meaning, out of any

context. But most important for the exegete was the idea that the literal level of meaning was that which told "what happened." In the case of Moses leading the children of Israel out of Egypt, the literal level is history, a recorded event from the past. An event's being history enabled the interpreter to distinguish between it and parables, exemplary tales not possessing a literal or historical meaning. Beyond history is the spiritual significance of an event, itself divisible into three levels, the first of which is the allegorical, in which the historical event is seen as a prefiguration or type for another event (Moses leading the children of Israel out of Egypt is a prefiguration of Jesus leading mankind out of perdition). As Robert Hollander says of this process, "The *letters* of Scripture, when reporting events, have the peculiar quality of being able to signify words which simultaneously signify facts, which facts also simultaneously are figures, types, or shadows (*umbrae*) of other facts."[1] The moral level of interpretation is somewhat vaguer, usually relating to the faith; the Moses story might be an admonition to keep faith in extreme adversity. The fourth level, the anagogical or mystical, relates the event to God's plan for the flow of cosmic history, teleology; its message might be that the faithful shall be saved. Thus we have history, morality, and metaphysics bound up in a single text.

Sarduy's text puts literature on the same level as Scripture, that is, Sarduy puts all texts on the same level, the sacred being a contribution by the reader. The method of fourfold allegorical interpretation may therefore grant the reader access to the work, with some alterations. First, the literal level of meaning (always remembering that the use of the word *level* is merely a convenient figure, that all levels of meaning occur at the surface of the text): the literal or historical level here is the history of language, the chronicle of how words change identity over time. This is taken up in the Ensor-inspired chapter "The Entry of Christ into Havana," which follows the section devoted to the development of Spanish on the Iberian Peninsula. This section is marked by a number of quotations from Hispano-Arabic poetry and references to Saint John of the Cross, quotations which constitute a synecdoche. We then follow the migration of Spanish to Cuba, where it undergoes further transformations. In order to define the process of Sarduy's text, we might rephrase Hollander's remark in this way: "The *letters* of Sarduy's text, when reporting events, have the peculiar quality of being able to signify words which simultaneously signify other words, which words also simultaneously are figures, types, or shadows (*umbrae*)—that is, metaphors—for other words." The moral level is not absent in Sarduy, but instead of referring to Christian metaphysics, it refers to the philosophy of Martin Heidegger, "the little stud from the Black Forest" (p. 21/241).[2] The anagogical or mystical level is likewise present, although in modified form: it refers us back again to the nature of language as a system of signs devoid of meaning, of interpretation as the individual's act of creating a meaning, a meaning found in or derived from himself, as in Heidegger's "hermeneutic circle."

Before pursuing the Heideggerian ramifications of Sarduy's text, we should recall its setting, Cuba. Not Cuba as it is (a geographical or political site), but a particular, peculiar Cuba, of which his language is a metaphor, in the same way that Cabrera Infante's language, in *Tres tristes tigres*,[3] aspires to be a metaphor for another Cuba. In his ironic (in the way Eliot's notes to *The Wasteland* are ironic) note to the book, Sarduy states: "Three cultures have superposed themselves one on another to constitute Cuban culture—the Spanish, the African, and the Chinese; three fictions that allude to each of them make up this book" (p. 151/328). Cuba is a trinitarian (at first) reality, but there is also the mysterious fourth element, referred to as "The Unnamable Bald Female" (p. 20/241). This is, of course, Death, the death alluded to in Tocqueville's comparison of New England and the tropics, the death lurking just below the glittering surface of Carribean nature. The history of language has also (wrongly) been seen as a history of decay: Latin "decays" into the modern Romance languages. Sarduy plays with this fictitious history of decay in his history of Spanish and its cubanization in order to incorporate political history into linguistic history. The advent of the Spaniards was an act of violence, just as the history of Cuba is a movement of violence from east to west across the island. This would include Fidel Castro, whose entrance into Havana is alluded to in the chapter called "The Entry of Christ into Havana." Violence, decay, and death are all involved with the tropics, are all aspects of language (from various points of view), and are some of the motifs that give unity to the text.

Four is a number to which we must return as we again consider the first chapter of the book, "Curriculum Cubense," a Cuban course of study (and also the idea of a race). First we have a rather taut exchange between two characters (and we should always keep in mind the idea of character as letter, or the Spanish word for character, *personaje*, as *persona* or mask), Auxilio and Socorro. These names are synonyms as well as being two of the many names of the Virgin, as is the Dolores who appears later. These ladies are versions (deconsecrated to be sure) of the Virgin as vessel, seen here as lacking content. They are the signs of language, the signifiers chasing after or searching in vain for meaning. Auxilio is undergoing an "identity crisis" (understandably) because she has none, except as a searcher-for-identity, a role which links her to Heidegger's *Dasein* (his term for that aspect of humanity involved in inquiries into and investigations of its own mode of being). Socorro responds to Auxilio's outburst (p. 11/235) by telling her to drop dead, to cease to exist either as a thing (Heidegger's ontic mode) or as being, the ontological mode. Auxilio retorts with a modified quotation from the sonnet "Love Constant beyond Death" by the Spanish baroque poet Francisco de Quevedo: she makes the subject of the clause "I" where the original was "my soul": "Seré ceniza, mas tendré sentido" (I shall be ash, but I shall have awareness). It should be recalled also that the expression "tendré sentido" may also mean "I shall have meaning," an idea that converts the verse into a restatement of Saint Augustine's idea that language is born out of desire: what keeps Auxilio alive is her hope (hence the future tense of the verb), her will-to-meaning, seen in the text as the longing of the mystics for union with God. This God (meaning) is referred to in a duet the two females sing as

> Always absent, always absent,
> He does evil gratuitously.
> (P. 12/235)

The evil he does is merely to exist, to remind the signs of their emptiness: "For the signifier is a unit in its very uniqueness, being by nature symbol only of an absence."[4]

In this introductory phase of the text, Sarduy dramatizes the plight of the signs: they long for (mystic) union with meaning, referred to as a God or other masculine figure. This introduces the erotic element implicit in the relationship between masculine and feminine, the same erotic relationship expressed in sacred terms in mystic poetry, particularly that of Saint John of the Cross. A twist is given to this eroticism, one already suggested by Saint John's relationship with God: the names of the signs, Auxilio and Socorro, while seeming to refer to female characters, are masculine in gender. This hetero-homosexual play reinforces the ludic aspect of the whole text; it is a carnival of language, literally a "farewell to the flesh" in which the reader is led to see that words are only surfaces, that whatever meaning desire imputes to the signs, they will forever be mere shells tricked out in whatever costumes fit the occasion (the context). The baroque concept of *desengaño* is the metaphor that best explains the situation: the drama of the signs, their being doomed to a permanent state of emptiness, their being condemned to exist as surfaces, points out to the reader that what is at stake in the text is language itself, that there is nothing hidden here, that the surface, or a palimpsestlike series of surfaces, is all.

It is precisely because of this rhetorical consistency that *De donde son los cantantes* is so outwardly baffling. Instead of being introduced to an allegorical or metaphorical situation by stages, as he is, say, in *Morel* or, as we shall see, in Cortázar's *Rayuela*, the reader here is plunged directly into the middle of things. Depending on one's position, this is either to disregard the reader completely or to treat him with unaccustomed respect. What is demanded of the reader, and again we might bear Dante in mind, is that he share the writer's culture, in this case that he know something about linguistics and twentieth century philosophy, just as Dante could demand of his readers that they share his familiarity with theology. Unlike Dante or Bioy, Sarduy does not mask his allegory with a plot. *De donde son los cantantes*, whose radical of presentation is metaphoric recurrence, transmits its ideas by repeating its various metaphorical dramas again and again, by agglomerating those dramas. To read the text is, necessarily, to reread it, in the same way that a "reading" of myths is a reading of all available permutations of myths.

Sarduy has been termed a neobaroque writer,[5] and there can be no doubt that because of his reiteration of elements of Spanish baroque culture—the poetry of Góngora, Quevedo, and Saint John or his (ironic) utilization of the idea of "passion" and other religious-erotic concepts—he is. But it might be more fruitful to associate him with a "Spanish" writer of an earlier period, Prudentius (348–415?), since *De donde son los cantantes* resembles the *Psychomachia* in so many ways. Prudentius's allegorical poem on the struggle between virtues and vices cannot be subjected to the fourfold exegetical technique because it patently lacks a literal level, and yet because of its majestic stylization, its wealth of significant detail, and its ritualized accumulation of scenes, it reminds one of Sarduy's text. It is the utter strangeness of the drama enacted in both texts that links them, a strangeness which repels psychological identification on the part of the reader.

This depersonalization of character, the association of characters and ideas, and the absolute disregard of anything even resembling a plot or any other form of temporal organization that would make the text "lifelike" connects Sarduy's work with satire. When we realize that the narrative represents, talks about, and is a metaphor only for its own processes and that these elements are a part of language taken as a totality, we see just how futile a reading of the text as any other sort of literary phenomenon would be. To be sure, Sarduy includes references to Cuba, which is only natural since the language he is concerned with is his own Cuban Spanish, and it is here perhaps that we see a contamination of the kind of purity to which Sarduy's text aspires by historical circumstance. Similarly, when he alludes to figures from the "real world," such as Jacques Lacan or Martin Heidegger, he is including the nonliterary world in his text even if he might not want those allusions to constitute a link between the text and an extratextual reality. Within the text, the allusions act as reinforcements of narrative coherence, but their presence does point out a possible gap between the culture of the reader and that of the writer (or his text).

It is the reader's knowledge that connects any text to a cultural context, not the text itself: it is no doubt unfortunate that most readers lack the intimate knowledge of Ireland necessary to follow Joyce's references, the knowledge of Southern history to make an annotated Faulkner unnecessary, or a familiarity with French culture equivalent to Proust's. The same is true for those matters most important to Sarduy's text, but this gap between reader and writer does not mean that the text can only be read within the confines of a cultural framework. It is not only these so-called modern works which challenge the reader; a cursory reading of Dickens or George Eliot reveals a culture, often presented in terms of biblical and liturgical references, to which most modern readers have only the most limited access. Ignorance gives us easy entry to no literature, and it is perhaps the realization on the part of the authors considered in this essay that they must educate their readers that constitutes what is truly modern in them. They demand what the nineteenth century obscured and what earlier centuries took for granted: a common culture shared by all educated people.

It is this intellectual distance between author and reader and text and reader which has gained the new Latin American narrative the reputation as an elitist literature. What has been forgotten is that all literature is elitist. The written word in Western culture has never been the property of all, although it has always been public property. It belongs to those who are willing to work at it, regardless of social or economic class. But there is, along with the need to make allusions to extratextual matters, a tacit confession that the reader may not know who or what is being alluded to, together with a tacit hope that the reader will find out; and this puts the concept of the literary text as a hermetically sealed system into some doubt. The one text in the Latin American canon which takes up this matter of allusion most seriously is Julio Cortázar's *Rayuela*, a work that shows off its complexity as it hastens to explain itself.

6

Julio Cortázar
Self-explanation &
Self-destruction

Julio Cortázar's *Rayuela* (1963),[1] the work that put both its author and Spanish American literature into a position of prominence in Western culture, is a deliberately essayistic text. It attempts to enact a coming to grips with the problem faced by all authors, the relationship between what the author talks about and how he talks about it. The *it* in the writings we have considered until this point, the dominant metaphor, has been, variously, of an esthetic, linguistic, or psychomoral nature. Bioy Casares's works deal, strictly speaking, with esthetic matters—the creation of an author, the purely verbal identity of any narrator—while Sarduy's narrative deals with the existential problem of language itself. Machado de Assis's writings deal with personalities, the warped personalities of vices incarnate which have been the satirist's stock in trade for centuries. Cortázar's book, eclectic in so many other senses, is eclectic also in this one: it dramatizes the problem any author faces when he writes—which elements he will select and which reject, and how he will use those he selects, whatever elements his culture supplies to him. At the same time, Cortázar represents the same sort of problem, the dialectical or nondialectical relationship of "tradition and the individual talent," on a philosophical level by creating a protagonist who tries to evade a life of preordained patterns.

The metaphorical relationship between *Rayuela*'s two sides, the conscious mirroring of the ethical and the esthetic, is further

complicated by the protagonist's also being his own narrator.[2]
That is, the text simultaneously writes and "unwrites" itself as it
grows. A word might be said about the two reading methods
offered to the reader at the beginning of *Rayuela:* the reader may
choose to follow either the "Tablero de Dirección" or to read the
text as an ordinary book (or, if he disdains both options, invent
his own reading method). If he chooses the short reading, he
omits the chapters designated "From Other Sides/Omissible
Chapters." Immediately the reader is challenged by the text: to
choose the easy, "feminine" (in Cortázar's terminology) route or
to choose the complex, possibly baffling route seemingly
suggested by the text itself. This is a kind of existentialist
"either/or" tempest in a teapot which plays not only on the
reader's self-esteem but also on his snobbery (who would admit
to having chosen the feminine plan and abandoned a third of
the book?). Notwithstanding this crux, it is advisable to read the
book both ways and then experiment, simply to see how Cortázar's sense of composition works, how what is disarticulated
neatly in the long reading is rather ambiguously articulated in
the short reading.

Articulation is indeed the dominant metaphor in *Rayuela:* how
a character imagines his life to be defective because the pieces do
not cohere as he would like, and how Cortázar would like to
break down a traditional plot by fusing it with meditations on
narrative problems. It is rather like a cubist still life in which we
see all sides of a given object at the same time, something impossible except in the work of art. But let us note at the same
time that Cortázar's experiment is not without precedents.
Saporta's *Composition No. 1* and Huxley's *Eyeless in Gaza* are also
forays into new forms of discourse. What we have in *Rayuela* is a
melange derived from Breton's *Nadja*, Sartre's *La Nausée*, Beckett's *Murphy*, with a touch of Céline's *Voyage au bout de la nuit*,
reworkings all of the story of the soul's journey to enlightenment, of the same kind we find in Apuleius's *Golden Ass* or
Bonaventura's *Itinerarium Mentis in Deum*. Cortázar, following
Breton and Sartre, develops this model on a less obviously religious plane (although it is nevertheless a religious plot) and
combines it with esthetic speculation. To what end? The clearest

object in view is the reader himself, whose views on literature and life Cortázar has long been trying to change.[3]

Cortázar's dissatisfaction with the status quo, or what he imagines the status quo to be, of occidental narrative, what he consistently calls "the novel," has been long lived. In fact, his earliest utterances on "the novel"[4] are testimonies of this dissatisfaction. But there is more to the situation than esthetic impatience. In reality Cortázar is a genuine sufferer from what Harold Bloom has called the "anxiety of influence."[5] Simply stated, this anxiety, which Bloom sees operative in all modern poetry, is caused by the unavoidable influence of the poets of the past on the creative ability of later writers. There is no moment of their work which is not warped by a backward glance at their "forefathers," and the result of this constant rearguard action is *"a history of anxiety and self-saving caricature, of distortion, of perverse, willful revisionism without which modern poetry as such could not exist"* (p. 30; italics in original). Modern writers, to rephrase Bloom's thesis, are born with oedipal problems which they resolve in the ways just described.

Without seeing Cortázar in the light of the anxiety of influence theory, it is difficult to understand just what it is he finds so oppressive about the literature, specifically the narrative literature, of the past. What he calls the traditional novel is something that exists, if at all, only marginally in English and American literature and seems peculiarly French. In fact, Cortázar's attitude as an avant-garde writer seems almost to be a serious rendition of the ironic distinctions Borges makes between French and English literary history in "The Paradox of Apollinaire."[6] In that essay, Borges notes that French literature seems to be a product of French literary history, that instead of being written by people, it consists of "schools, manifestos, generations, avant-gardes, rearguards, lefts, rights, cells, and references to the tortuous destiny of Captain Dreyfus" (p. 48). Cortázar too looks at the novel (without ever distinguishing between the major genres) in the same way. There are good writers, of whom he approves, and bad ones, whose work he attacks. The major object of his literary assaults is the mythical "traditional novel," analagous to the one Ortega attacks in *The*

Dehumanization of Art. It is clear that Cortázar needs a straw man so that he can overcome his anxiety of influence, just as he needs a mythical "good-father" author, one, naturally, he creates himself, the novelist Morelli in *Rayuela.*

The creation of a "father" by an author is an act which ought to have elicited a torrent of critical speculation. The opposite is in fact true, and the sad reality of most Cortázar criticism is its pious repetition of what the author or his surrogate (Morelli) says about literature. Criticism becomes repetition. Morelli does have, however, a significance beyond Cortázar's own immediate need for a master. He is the master absent from Hispanic culture in general (especially since Spanish Americans, like their Peninsular counterparts, scrupulously avoid reading Brazilian or Portuguese authors, thereby excluding Machado de Assis or Eça de Queiroz from their spectrum). The single Spanish author who might, through sheer output, have vied for such a place of honor, Pérez Galdós, is held up to ridicule by Cortázar. In chapter 34 of *Rayuela*, the protagonist, Horacio Oliveira, reads a passage from *Lo prohibido*, and the text is so arranged that one line of Galdós is followed by a line of Oliveira's thoughts. The juxtaposition is ironic, and Galdós suffers, perhaps unjustly, in the process.

The creation of Morelli is important also because Cortázar not only shows him as a text (the characters comment on his works) but also as a character. One thinks of Plato's relationship with Socrates, the often commented control the younger philosopher had over his master when he turned him into a character. Perhaps Cortázar is showing something more than he realizes: if Morelli is a master, he is more like Cortázar himself than any living figure. And if this is true, he is relegating himself to the position of innovator, one who writes for the history of literature, and not necessarily to be read. To a certain extent this is true. *Rayuela* has aged, not so much in its abstract sense as an experiment with discourse, but in its style and its cultural accouterments. It is in this sense a rather banal *summa* of the early 1950s, existentialism-cum-mysticism. Borges's remark in the Apollinaire essay about the fact that, although Apollinaire and Rilke are of the same generation, Rilke's work seems fresh while Apollinaire's has become a collection of period pieces, holds true

for Cortázar as well. To write in order to change the "now" of
literature is to situate oneself prominently at the beginning of
another "now."

It is therefore in a double perspective that we should consider
Rayuela: what it did as a phenomenon in literary history remains;
what its accomplishments are as a work of art remain to be seen.
Above all else, *Rayuela* altered the sociological status of the
Spanish American writer. The Spanish American writer of the
1960s became almost as great a celebrity as his political counterparts. To be sure, writers of an earlier generation, such as
Neruda or Borges, were famous, as were such poets as Octavio
Paz or César Vallejo, but the publication of *Rayuela* inaugurated
a period of wide dissemination and, more importantly, of wide
exposure of writers to a primarily Spanish American public. Cortázar's text was an international Latin American success and
broke down barriers which long kept, for example, Mexican
readers from sharing reading experiences with Argentine
readers.

A serious obstacle fell, the idea that in order to be understood
by the Spanish speaking world in general a writer had to use a
kind of B.B.C. Spanish. *Rayuela* is an Argentine book in the way
Cabrera Infante's *Tres tristes tigres* is a Cuban book or Guimarães
Rosa's *Grande Sertão: Veredas* is a Brazilian book. This is a step
perhaps difficult to understand for an Anglo-American audience. Faulkner was not, we assume, afraid of not being understood by Scotch readers. Something may be lost, but how much
more was lost when writers had to become grammarians to
produce a work of art? No longer would a writer hesitate to use
either localisms or street talk of any sort.

The relaxation on the linguistic level has its counterpart on the
sexual plane as well. Cortázar's characters talk about sex, practice it with an almost Henry Miller–like verve, and regard it as a
part of everyday life. This frankness was not common in the
Spanish American world before 1963. There were exceptions of
course, but, again, Cortázar's text made sex into a subject for all
Spanish American writers, a matter which no longer had to be
treated elliptically. That this corresponds to a change in the attitude of the reading public (and is not therefore a cause *per se*) is
a matter for consideration. It would seem, as Emir Rodríguez

Monegal states in his study of the "Boom," that Cortázar and the social change mutually complemented each other.[7]

Important for the non–Latin American reader of Cortázar is the kind of culture Cortázar displays. Borges and Bioy Casares had spattered their texts with allusions and quotations, but Cortázar carries this display of cultural material to an absurd point. Like a baroque writer of the seventeenth century, Cortázar stuffs his text with references; his characters talk about religion, philosophy, art, literature, and history in a professional way, as if their lives were spent in galleries and libraries. At the same time, this manifestation of culture, though accomplished by an international cast, seems very Argentinian, indeed, very Latin American. To "know" French, English, and American literature is not rare in Latin American middle-class life, and an educated Argentinian would not shock his friends by referring to Baudelaire. At the same time, this same person would be familiar with his own literature, so that Cortázar can refer to Raymond Roussel, Musil, and Roberto Arlt in the same passage without hestitating. It is this, for us, bizarre mixture—which we find in Borges as well—that makes *Rayuela* seem so dazzling. At the same time, the tendency toward the encyclopedic is typical of satire, so that in a sense culture and genre complement each other in a quite natural way.

The idea that culture is nothing more than a skin, a surface that desensitizes and isolates the bearer, is taken up in *Rayuela* during the Parisian phase of Horacio Oliveira's life. The myriad possibilities that present themselves to Oliveira, the conflicting religions, philosophies, and literary schools are proof to him that he will not find what he wants through them. This situation is Augustinian in origin in that illumination, the kind of ontological security Oliveira seeks, is something given, not something acquired. In other terms, Oliveira is seeking grace, which cannot be acquired through works alone. The Paris section of his life is therefore a progressive discarding of his cultural baggage, a separation from his milieu, which includes his friends and his lover, Maga, the Nadja of *Rayuela*.

This renunciation is accomplished through a series of parallel deaths, suicides, and sacrifices which make most of the characters in Paris doubles for Oliveira. The death of Rocamadour,

Maga's child, the event which precipitates Oliveira's banish-
ment from Paris, is the symbolic death of Oliveira's humanity,
the side of him that arouses pity in others. At the same time,
Morelli is dying in a hospital, and another of Olivera's lovers,
Pola, is dying of cancer. These deaths underline the mind-body
dichotomy which puts arbitrary limits on the protagonist's
search, and, at the same time, they make him aware of his need
to die in one sense in order to be reborn. Again, the text is a
chronicle of how an individual passes from one state to another:
in Machado, Brás Cubas is reborn in his text; in Bioy a man dies
so that a text may be born; and here in Cortázar a fictitious but
exemplary life is transformed into words on a page.

Oliveira's most significant renunciation, the one of which he
repents almost immediately, is his giving up Maga, the woman
he loves. This enactment of the idea that one always destroys
what one loves most is extremely important to Oliveira because
it makes manifest his desire for salvation, no matter what the
cost. Again, the parallel to Augustine in this sundering of personal ties to the world in order to save one's soul is clear. Since
Maga cannot give him what he wants (although she seems to
possess it), she must be sacrificed. In the same way, when he
feels his enlightenment is at hand, Oliveira does not hestitate to
use his friend and spiritual double, Traveler, as a means to reach
it. Whether he does in fact reach his goal is not clear, but it is the
goal that justifies the process and the sacrifices.

There is certainly nothing new, either in content or in style, in
Oliveira's history. We must then turn to the other side of the text
in order to see what made it so explosive. And, again, if we look
carefully here, we shall see that the interpolation of material alien
to the protagonist's story (though related to it thematically) is not
new at all. The kind of moralizing digressions in Mateo Alemán's
Guzmán de Alfarache or Defoe's *Robinson Crusoe*[8] parallel the various sorts of interpolations Cortázar utilizes. His book does not
disorder plot, not even the epic sense of beginning *in medias res;* it
simply makes the straight line into an arabesque.

Plot may be understood either as an element of the work of art
or as an aspect of the psychology of composition. In the first
sense, plot is the arrangement of events; strictly speaking, their
arrangement to show causality. This does not, as Aristotle or

Borges would have us believe, mean that paratactic texts like the
Golden Ass or the *Lazarillo de Tormes* are not "plotted." They obey a
different order, one in which causality is generally removed from
the realm of ordinary human logic and left in the hands of fate or a
divinity. They follow a process of accumulation which leads to
some sort of culminating moment, a hierophany in the *Golden
Ass*, an ironic discovery of identity in the *Lazarillo*. We might also
note that in *La Nausée*, the same sort of trajectory is found.

Rayuela displays two sorts of organization, the type we see in
Sartre's text, and another, one in which the reader "sees" the
author selecting those elements which will constitute the book's
"best of all possible worlds." Oliveira's story is that of Roquentin; the text's own "story" is its assimilation of all sorts of
heterogeneous material (newspaper clippings, almanac quotations, passages from other literary texts). The reader may not be
"correct" in his utilization of the materials Cortázar has brought
together under the one roof of the text, correct here being
merely an approximation of the author's own wishes. But these
wishes are irrelevant because the mere act of assemblage suffices
as *prima facie* evidence of a wish to create an order. Despite the
ironic quotation from Bataille's *Haine de la poésie* (chapter 136)
about the author's own inability to explain why he brought together certain materials, the fact remains that the materials have
been gathered. They are now in the hands of the reader, whose
reading will connect the pieces. All plots are "replotted" by the
reading, which accounts for all loose ends.

Cortázar seems to have overlooked this aspect of reading in
his desire to work some sort of disordering magic on the reader's
sensibility. Like the surrealists, whose work he has long ad-
mired, he forgets that interpretation is a weapon which turns
the text against its creator. Like the monster in Mary Shelley's
Frankenstein, the work, once in the world, acquires characteris-
tics unimagined by the creator. It may horrify or delight him, but
it will no longer be his property. What Cortázar wishes,
therefore, is not something an artifact can give: he wants to
change his reader, but he uses a tool that the reader will twist
into something different. Whatever changes occur in the reader
as he reads will be modified when the work is reconstructed in

memory. There it will be organized and transformed, turned into an image of the reader's, not the artist's, mind.

What happens to *Rayuela* reminds us of what has happened to the didactic satires of the eighteenth century. When we read Swift or Voltaire, it is obvious we are not reading them as their original readers did. We see simultaneously more and less in both texts than did their age. Does Voltaire really teach us anything? Perhaps, but the thrust of his philosophical arguments is meaningful only to those readers who can reconstruct the extratextual milieu that surrounded *Candide* when it first appeared. *Gulliver's Travels* (which even had a different title) is more a hallucinatory experience for today's readers, more an anatomy of the soul than a satire directed against specific targets. The error of Cortázar's didacticism is its naïve faith in the ability of the work of art to retain his intentions when placed in alien hands. To be sure, *Rayuela* should be read as one of Stanley Fish's *self-consuming artifacts:* "A self-consuming artifact signifies most successfully when it fails, when it points *away* from itself to something its forms cannot capture. If this is not anti-art, it is surely anti-art-for-art's sake because it is concerned less with the making of better poems than with the making of better persons,"[9] but the question of whether Cortázar's enterprise is worth the trouble or not remains unanswered. To read him fairly we must forget the banality of his ideas and consider the goals he sets both for himself and for us.

He fails, perhaps, but there is grandeur in his failure. The experiment with narrative, the attempt to point out what might be done with narrative, and the risks involved—all of this constitutes a noble endeavor. Whatever else *Rayuela* may have done, it certainly made the Latin American literary world aware of new possibilities. A good example of the kind of book Latin America was prepared for by *Rayuela* is Cabrera Infante's *Tres tristes tigres*. This is in no way a suggestion that Cabrera Infante is a follower or imitator of Cortázar. Far from it. And yet, when we realize that *Tres tristes tigres* is an assemblage, a kind of verbal scrapbook, then we must inevitably recall Cortázar's art of assemblage in *Rayuela*.

Rayuela must also be remembered whenever language, narra-

tive structure, or the depiction of the artist within the work of art
are discussed. *Rayuela* is a point of crystalization for so many
subjects that one is tempted to set it at the head of a movement.
This of course would be a falsification. Authors like Machado de
Assis, Bioy Casares, Roberto Arlt, Juan Carlos Onetti, and Felis-
berto Hernández, dead, forgotten or simply ignored for one
reason or another, all did what Cortázar did. His importance lies
in having done it all at the moment when he was able to make a
huge impression on a new generation of readers and writers.
Drawing lines between the writers of different generations is not
difficult, especially in Latin America where two genres, satire
and to a lesser extent romance have held such sway. That is,
since most writers are working within the confines of a single
genre, the essential traits of that genre soon begin to be common
currency. What *Rayuela* is, then, is not so much an innovation as
a gathering place in which an entire catalog of innovations is put
on display.

To see just what the post-*Rayuela* era is in terms of the structure of the text, we shall examine Cabrera Infante's *psychomachia*,
Tres tristes tigres. What we shall find is a book which takes for
granted the reader's ability to see the text as a whole (again,
having to read it twice instead of once) from the outset. What
Joseph Frank said of Joyce, "Joyce cannot be read—he can only
be reread,"[10] is true of most of the large-scale satires and romances being produced in Latin America today. The work can
only be apprehended in its totality when memory is capable of
fitting all the pieces together. This is only possible when the text
has already become familiar. In much the same way, the authors
of these texts somehow suppose, as did Faulkner, that the
reader has knowledge of unwritten texts.[11] That is, the demands put upon the reader extend beyond requiring detailed
familiarity with one text; they extend to the author's entire
oeuvre.

Guillermo Cabrera
Infante
The Vast Fragment

While Cabrera Infante does not share Cortázar's didactic attitude toward literature, their texts, *Tres tristes tigres* and *Rayuela*,
are remarkably similar in that they overwhelm the reader with
an avalanche of fragments, pieces which only cohere after memory links them. Cabrera Infante, unlike Cortázar, does not feel
impelled to instruct: he assumes the existence of a public that
will appreciate his scrapbook technique and his depiction of a
lost milieu. This public would share the archeological tastes of
the readers of Joyce or Proust, and would not be jarred by the
discontinuities of satire or the need to have a familiarity with
pre-Castro Havana. The reader of Latin American satire is under
great pressure; to read a book like *Tres tristes tigres* (1968) he
must not only know a great deal but must also hold his own
literary expectations in abeyance, paying close attention to the
text's own rhetoric. Only by determining a work's "intrinsic
genre" can the reader ever hope to read it fairly, and such a
reading will result, in the case of Latin American narrative, in an
esthetics of narrative based on satire.

But such an esthetic is unfortunately not the one generally
being used to read Latin American narrative. It is as though an
entire world of critics were suffering from a critical malaise, one
which Paul de Man, in another context, calls "the rhetoric of
blindness."[1] De Man describes a situation in which critics do
something other than what they propose to do as they practice
their particular arts on literary texts. It is de Man's contention

that the reader of these critics is in the privileged position of being able to "see" beyond their avowed intentions and to profit from their blindness. That the reader is himself blind in some way de Man takes as a matter of course, adding that there is no cure for this malady. The importance of "criticizing the critic," then, is propaedeutic: de Man's blind critics (Lukács, Poulet, Blanchot) fail in ways that may make the perspicacious reader at least take his blindness into account.

A reader blind to the satiric identity of *Tres tristes tigres*, expecting to find in it a novelistic analysis of Cuba on the eve of revolution, might be tempted to condemn the book. From the point of view of a novel-centered esthetics, satire is juvenile: it lacks psychological depth, it lacks coherence, and it is usually packed with what seems to the novel reader useless information. And if literary criticism is equated with valorization, with the novel taken as the highest level in a hierarchy of narrative, then the conclusions are correct.

Such is in fact the opinion of John Updike, who reviewed the English translation of *Tres tristes tigres* in *The New Yorker*.[2] Updike's expectations regarding Cabrera Infante's text seem to have been multiple. Early in the review he states, "An American reader, especially now that Cuba is remoter than China, longs for a more anatomical portrait of this Havana that has vanished" (p. 91), but we wonder what an "American reader's" longings can have to do with Cabrera Infante's book, which was not, presumably, written to satisfy the desires of an American audience. A more mysterious expression of disappointment appears toward the end of the review where he notes that Latin American writers such as Machado de Assis and García Márquez have produced "adventurously original novels" (p. 93), an assertion which seems aimed at making us ask ourselves, "If they were adventurously original, why didn't Cabrera Infante follow their example?"

Updike's expectations as a reader are more important to the goals of this essay than his opinions of *Tres tristes tigres*, and we may all profit from his blindness. We might rephrase his novel-centered evaluation in this way: would a reviewer of American fiction in Bombay expect every narrative written about life in the United States during the 1960s and early 70s to contain refer-

ences to the war in Indochina or the presidency of Richard Nixon?
He might, if he were like John Updike in expecting all long
narratives to be novels, with the novel's interest in history. It
might happen that America could be analyzed by means of a
satirical depiction of its customs and institutions, such as the
one in Thomas Pynchon's *The Crying of Lot 49* (1966). Pynchon's
satire cannot be judged according to novelistic criteria, and to
call it a failure because it does not meet novelistic expectations
would be absurd.

Updike's assertion that Machado de Assis and García Márquez are good and that Cabrera Infante is bad is, of course, only
a matter of personal preference. His choice of comparisons for
Cabrera Infante is, in the context of this essay, rather ironic since
all three work within the same genre even though their texts are
so very different. All use dominant metaphors drawn from different sources: Machado is concerned with madness, García
Márquez writes about the need for fiction to have endings, and
Cabrera Infante deals with permutations of betrayal. But all
write metaphoric texts, texts about an idea, not about people
involved in the process of history.

However, all of Updike's criticisms of *Tres tristes tigres* derive
from an association even more telling than his disappointment
that Cabrera Infante's text is not a novel about pre-Castro
Havana. Updike dislikes *Tres tristes tigres* because "its excite-
ment derived from the translation of the methods of *Ulysses* into
Cuban idiom, and that, restored to Joyce's mother tongue, it
shows up as a tired copy" (p. 91). Updike then forges a detailed
comparison of the two books:

> wandering itineraries are mapped street by street, minor char-
> acters reappear in a studied interweave, a variety of voices
> abruptly soliloquize, a kind of "Oxen of the Sun" proces-
> sion of literary parodies is worked on the theme of Trotsky's
> assassination, an endless "Nighttown" drunkenness episode
> picks up the deliberate hung-over banality of the Eumaeus
> sequence, and a female interior monologue closes the book.
> (P. 91)

If *Tres tristes tigres* were a copy of *Ulysses* (it is actually derived
from Petronius's *Satyricon*[3]), Updike's comparison might have

been devastating, but in fact none of the scenes in the Cuban text supposedly taken from *Ulysses* even vaguely resembles its "counterpart" in Joyce's great satire: the "female interior monologue" at the end of *Tres tristes tigres* Updike imagines modeled on Molly Bloom's soliloquy is the transcription Silvestre, the author-character, makes of a madwoman's ravings—and the madwoman's words appear in the text only because Silvestre mentions to another character that he had once copied down the discourse of such a person. It is there because it too is part of Silvestre's life in Havana. The real purpose of the comparison would seem to be to juxtapose two texts Updike dislikes, texts rendered identical by his displeasure. Why he despises *Ulysses*, which he calls "static and claustrophobic" (static being a word he also applies to *Tres tristes tigres*) (p. 93) is unclear, although it may, again, be the difficulties a novel-centered reader has with understanding satire.

Updike is blind to the fact that *Tres tristes tigres* (unlike *Ulysses*) has no plot. It is an assemblage, a scrapbook kept by Silvestre made up of his version of what others have said. Its chronology is necessarily broken up and fragmentary because it follows no particular story. This aspect of the text is particularly manifest in the section entitled "Bachata" (chapter 13), where Silvestre says, "It was then, exactly at that moment (which I shall never forget, and so that it will be that way, I jotted down these notes when I got home) that I saw the bubble in the windshield. I don't know if you know, you on the other side of the page, that automobile window glass is made of two transparent sheets of glass of identical thickness separated by a sheet of invisible plastic" (p. 344/373).[4] Here is the book speaking to the reader, explaining itself through a character. What we have is Silvestre's raw material (as his friend Arsenio Cué notes on p. 404/439 when he asks Silvestre if he is going to write down their conversation), the pieces he has managed to salvage of his life in Havana during a certain period of time. When Cortázar has a narrator relate Morelli's attitude toward composition, he might be talking about *Tres tristes tigres*:

> Somewhere Morelli tried to justify his narrative incoherencies by asserting that the lives of others, as they come to us in so-called reality, come not as movies but as photographs, that

is, we cannot take in the action but only its Eleatically clipped fragments. There is nothing more than the minutes in which we are with that other person or when he tells us what happened to him or when he projects for us what he has to do. At the end there remains a photo album, filled with fixed instants; never "becoming" taking place before us, the step from yesterday to today, the first needle of oblivion in our memory. (P. 532/382)

This is the kind of articulation Cortázar imagined and Cabrera Infante put into practice.

The insight to which Updike leads us in his blindness is the impossibility of coming to any text with expectations of any sort. While this may seem to be a lesson so elementary as to be trivial, especially since we know we cannot escape from our subjectivity, we must make an effort to realize that there is more to fiction than the novel. Updike incarnates the demons Cortázar calls the "traditional novel" and the "feminine reader," devils one might have hoped to have been exorcised by now. The tradition to which Cabrera Infante belongs, and this too, granted, is a kind of valorization, is that of Petronius, Sterne, Lewis Carroll, Céline, James Purdy, and Thomas Pynchon. Like Pynchon and Céline, Cabrera Infante is pessimistic, more interested in caricature than in character, more eschatologically than historically oriented. Updike has done all readers of Latin American satire a great service: his refusal to see the text, his unwillingness to adjust his reading to his subject, his novel-centered sensibility are all warning signs we must all heed if we wish to read these texts on their own terms.

The reader's first task in dealing with *Tres tristes tigres* is reconstruction. He begins by reassembling the text, making sense of what appears to be an agglomeration. He connects the pieces of the characters' lives as they appear in the text, like a quilt-maker constructing a whole out of scraps, until suddenly he sees a kind of nebulous totality, a whole fragment which points to a vast number of new totalities.

Tres tristes tigres, like *Brás Cubas* or *Morel*, is another elegiac text. Like the early poetry of Borges, it is concerned with documenting a loss, not only of the object observed but of the observer as well. Cabrera Infante, unlike Bioy, is not as overtly concerned with the phoenix-like death-and-resurrection of the work of art out of the ashes of life, perhaps because he (like his characters) realizes that the two worlds, though tangential, are eternally separate. The world to which the text corresponds is dead, and the text can only be a metaphor, a reality of words with no specific reference to anything palpable.

The basic metaphor on which *Tres tristes tigres* is constructed is the notion that esthetic representation is a betrayal. The work of art cannot be about anything but itself, and since it is a translation of one mode into another, it cannot presume to have any h᠎ 3her status than its subject. Cabrera Infante's satire is a study of the idea of betrayal, both as a form and as a content. That is, one kind of betrayal may be substituted for another: if a translator calls the lions of a particular text sea lions, he has violated a trust; if a friend has lied to his friend, he has broken a bond; if a text pretends to capture scenes from various lives but succeeds only in giving versions of those scenes, then it too has betrayed its "promise" to the "original."

The satirist is, of course, satirized[5] in Cabrera Infante's work. Silvestre, the putative "secretary of history," is his own subject. He must deform what he recalls of himself simply because of what the act of transcription entails. Silvestre is an implacable enemy of oblivion (he mentions this hatred on p. 287/309), and he is fully conscious of the inevitability of memory, the persistence of the past in its invasion of the present (p. 306/287), but he himself is defeated because he can only give the shell of what he observes. Like the fruit growing near the Dead Sea,[6] representation is a surface, devoid of real content, always promising something, always "about" something, but never anything. Within the text this emptiness, seen also as a kind of sterility, is reflected in the characters' constant word play.

Puns are a means whereby the characters generate the illusion of action. They create a verbal space, but this space is illusory because it is conceived in the mode of metaphor, of substitution, and not in the metonymic mode of flow. There is literally no place for the characters to go in the text because they have reached the end of their historical and cultural rope. Like Bioy's narrator, they are trapped on an island (Cuba here being as metaphoric as the island in *Morel*), and all their movement is

circular, reminiscent also of the protagonists' trajectories in
L'Immoraliste or *Voyage au bout de la nuit*. Like Bioy's narrator,
they too will become art, but it is the cost that receives the
emphasis here, a heavy price unmitigated by the love Bioy's narrator feels for Faustine. Individual salvation of the kind Bioy
postulates is a poor consolation for Cabrera Infante's characters
because it too is tainted by betrayal. There must be an interpreter, a Silvestre or the reader so often addressed by Silvestre.
Committing oneself to language, as Borges seems to be saying in
texts as disparate as "Borges and I" and "Tlön, Uqbar, Orbis
Tertius" confers a provisional immortality on the subject, but it
simultaneously subjugates the subject to the interpretations of
the reader.

Metaphoric space, which the characters create when they
make puns, and in which they reside after Silvestre writes down
his version of what he has experienced, is in reality no space at
all. It is for this reason that the characters exist only in each
other's company; they are all mirror images of one another,
reflections of reflections. Much is made of this in the relationship between Cué and Silvestre because other characters point
out their being twins, although they in no way resemble each
other physically. They constitute an ironic rejoinder to J. Hillis
Miller's statement about characters in the Victorian novel: "In
most Victorian novels the protagonist comes to know himself
and to fulfill himself by way of other people."[7] Cabrera Infante's
characters are shadows no amount of contact can complete.

This condition is exemplified in the text by the death of a
character who never actually appears. Bustrófedon, Cabrera Infante's Morelli, is a linguistic wizard, a pun master, and his
death provokes an immense crisis in the lives of the other
characters. They try to preserve his works (the parodic sequence
"The Death of Trotsky Told by Various Cuban Writers Years
After—or Before" is his), but, as the characters realize, his works
are not he. He is lost forever. Moreover, he becomes a character
in their memory, and finally becomes what they all become,
words. For the reader, Bustrófedon was never anything but language, and if we never experience him directly he is nonetheless
as "real" as Cué or Silvestre. His being absent is a sign of
the absence that underlies the existence of all the characters.

What Hillis Miller says about the novel (without ever clearly defining that elusive word) may be true: "A novel is a temporal rhythm made up of the movement of the minds of the narrator and his characters in their dance of approach and withdrawal, love and hate, convergence and divergence, merger and division" (p. 6), but we must remember at the same time that narrative temporality is linguistic. When the discourse stops, the text ends. Cabrera Infante's text is, or aspires to be, the language of a particular place and time, or at least his version of it, and its being enclosed in a book signifies its being dead. We shall see the text being used as a symbolic tomb in García Márquez's *Cien años de soledad* and José Donoso's *El obscene pájaro de la noche,* as in fact we have already seen it in *Morel.* For Cabrera Infante, however, the creation of the text, the verbal monument to the dead, is another betrayal, the act of having recourse to metaphor, because the actual subject is ephemeral. The text contains the ghost of ghosts, the remains of a language, itself a metaphor.

"Beguiling the hour" seems to be the principal occupation of Cabrera Infante's characters. They are dying with their milieu, like antediluvian beasts on the verge of extinction. Language is the only means left to them to dissimulate their despair. Like the digressions and interpolations in Greek romances, their verbal adventures give the illusion of expanding or widening time, but they are merely decorations. The world of *Tres tristes tigres* is sterile, except as the subject of a work of art, in the same way the world of Encolpius and Giton is a world which acknowledges itself to be without transcendence. Turning night into day, turning words inside out, being constantly in motion are all the means whereby Cabrera Infante's characters deceive themselves. It is just one more betrayal, one which leads both to death and to esthetic resurrection.

João Guimarães Rosa
Honneur des Hommes

Language as a sign of life, and linguistic play as a sign of fecundity are the hallmark of João Guimarães Rosa's *Grande Sertão: Veredas* (1956), one of the very few texts we shall consider which may be construed as optimistic. Language in *Grande Sertão* is a bridge between nature, the *sertão* (backlands), and culture and is used by men, who also constitute a bridge between the two worlds, both to name their artifacts and to imitate the sounds of the natural world. The narrator of the text, Riobaldo, continues the bridge metaphor by living on the edge of the backlands, a citizen both of nature and of culture. The effect of his bridge identity on his discourse is that of deformation, a condition in which we see the narrator mutilating and recreating the language he inherits from his society. There is no sense here that the turbulent, rural language of the narrator belongs to the past, in the way the *porteño* slang of *Rayuela*, or the Cuban Spanish of Cabrera Infante do when they intentionally evoke the language of a paritcular era, the 1950s in both of these cases. Language in Guimarães Rosa is the "honneur des hommes" of which Valéry speaks, not raw material to be sifted and purified, but natural energy which demonstrates man's dynamic status. Language here constantly reminds the reader that nothing in man is fixed, that while individuals and cultures have a personality and a continuity, they are nevertheless bound up in the ebb and flow of a universe in flux.

Grande Sertão argues against one of man's own inventions,

which the text takes to be man's worst enemy, linear time. When the flux of undifferentiated time or time taken as a series of recurrent cycles is transformed by man into linear history, he loses contact with a part of himself, the part belonging to nature. The great opposition in the text, Riobaldo's perpetual speculation about the existence of God and the Devil, is actually an erroneous representation of the difference between the world of culture and the world of nature. Riobaldo wonders if there is a Devil, although he never doubts the existence of God. For him the problem is one of morality, but for the reader the opposition is a false problem, since morality is not the text's principal subject. Instead of representing good and evil, God would seem to symbolize the universe as eternal, an essence, while the Devil stands for the world of phenomena (or language), the visible world of chaos and flux. While *Grande Sertão* might at first seem to recreate Pico della Mirandola's platonism, a system which shows how man participates in the lower world of flesh and how he may purge himself of base matter to become an angel, it is in fact an inversion of that system.

There are no hierarchies in *Grande Sertão*, because the text enacts the doctrines of Heraclitus in autobiographical form. Heraclitus's stress on the individual's need to comprehend the principles that govern both himself and his universe are represented metaphorically in Riobaldo's discourse by language itself, by the act of narrating. It is not what Riobaldo says but what he means that concerns the reader, not what he intends but what his discourse says through him. Riobaldo, virtually the "other" in Lacan's formula *"the unconscious is the discourse of the other,"*[1] is his own message. He is the *logos*, the reason or order of things representing itself for us, and he is, like all men in Heraclitus's sense, what he seeks. The dichotomy he senses, the split between God and the Devil, is really not a dichotomy but a basic principle of universal harmony, the harmony of opposites, of flux itself, which he expresses without comprehension. He reminds us several times, "The important thing is this: you listen to me, listen to me more than just listening to what I say; and listen disarmed" (p. 86/91),[2] or, "I don't know how to tell things in a straightforward way. I learned how to a little with my buddy Quelemém, but he sort of wants to know everything differently. He doesn't want the event itself, but the beyond-thing, the other thing" (p. 152/166).

These last two remarks would seem to be a restatement of Heraclitian fragment 50: "Listening not to me but to the Logos it is wise to agree that all things are one."[3] As usual, the utterance is paradoxical; we have no choice but to listen to the speaker, while at the same time we are required to interpret his words, to look beyond them. Riobaldo's advice also recalls fragment 93: "The lord whose oracle is in Delphi neither speaks out nor conceals, but gives a sign" (p. 211). *Grande Sertão* is a vast ideogram composed of language, containing an autobiography, yet standing as a huge metaphor about man's eternal condition. It demands elucidation because the articulation of its parts is confusing; but whatever values are assigned to those elements, one basic lesson is reiterated throughout: man is part of a cosmos in flux; he is not limited by history or circumstance, and his principal business in life should be to find the *logos*, the order of the universe, within himself. The microcosm is a metaphor for the macrocosm.

The *mise en scène* of this idea is strange and yet oddly familiar, especially for North American readers. Just as Melville used the first-person narrator and the world of whaling to deal with ethical and theological problems, Guimarães uses a first-person format and the *sertão* as his stage. Both the sailing ship and the *sertão* have the benefit of being *loci* divorced from historical contingency. They are isolated worlds within a macrocosm, and while their ultimate significance can only be seen in terms of the macrocosm, they use metaphors to express their ideas. Both *Moby Dick* and *Grande Sertão* utilize a setting derived from the world of romance; their characters too are heroic, just as the actions they describe are titanic in scale. *Grande Sertão* even resorts to such epic conventions as catalogs of warriors' names and councils of heroes in which decisions are made on the basis of what bards will sing about those present. All of this makes the vehicle of expression correspond to the high seriousness of the ideas at stake. Familiar problems are thrown into relief by being made strange and alien. Neither text is ironic and each attempts to make a statement about the human condition. Perhaps this is why the divorce from the "real world" of the novel and from the grotesque world of satire is necessary.

Of course, Riobaldo's tale is quite different from Ishmael's account of the Pequod's voyage. Whereas Ishmael's tale is about matters he witnesses and in which he participates marginally, Riobaldo's story is an autobiography. He makes the usual distinctions between the "I" narrator and the "I" actor usually formulated by picaresque narrators, but it is not his intention to confess his sins. Riobaldo is himself a truth which must be revealed, and it is for this reason the silent "o senhor" who listens, and in whose position we readers find ourselves, is so significant. This listener does not seem to be present in order to give absolution to the speaker, but rather to record his story. There are few references made to what it is the listener does as Riobaldo speaks, but one passage makes it clear: "Crossing of my life. Guarravacã—you look, you write" (p. 220/241). Riobaldo is not speaking figuratively here, and it would seem that we are to imagine the "learned" listener as a stenographer. It is tempting to identify him with Guimarães himself, recording the lessons gleaned from his sojourn in the backlands as a young doctor, but this association is of no special significance. The burden of interpretation lies with the reader, who must be diligent if he is to keep up simultaneously with the language and with the story Riobaldo tells.

Riobaldo's addresses to his public, beginning with his first words, tend to be soothing and adulatory, but his discourse is oddly ritualized: "A visit, here at home in my house, with me, lasts three days" (p. 22/19). Our visit in Riobaldo's house (the book itself) may last much longer than three days, but this magic number informs us that we are embarking on a rite of passage, from a kind of death (belief in linear history) to a resurrection, a realization that the world is in perpetual flux and that time moves in no single direction, an idea found also in the Cuban writer Alejo Carpentier's *El siglo de las luces*. Later Riobaldo puts us on our guard, "I tell things for myself; I tell things for you. When you don't understand me, wait for me" (p. 112/122), and again, "I tell you what I know and you don't know; but mainly I want to tell what I don't know that I know, and that maybe you know" (p. 175/192). The oracle is certainly speaking, urging us to keep up with him, not trying either to scare us away or to challenge us. Riobaldo is holding up a mirror to his audience throughout his discourse, but it is up to the reader to discern his own image.

The actual sequence of events in Riobaldo's life history reflects the message it propounds. Unlike Machado's Brás Cubas, Riobaldo does not worry about whether he should begin his autobiography at the end or the beginning: Guimarães resolves the problem of unity in the first person narrative, not by using a dead narrator, but by declaring constant change to be the only perspective. Riobaldo begins therefore nowhere, neither *in medias res* nor at one of the extremes. We have come to him, in some mysterious way, and in a similarly ambiguous fashion he will tell us what he has to say. He moves backwards and forwards through his past (and to this extent, his having a past, he is like traditional narrators), remembering in both directions, letting his story meander from one topic to another, imitating the Heraclitian rivers that run through the narrative.

The paradoxical mixture of metonymy and metaphor at the root of all narrative is almost bewildering here. In the first paragraph Riobaldo mentions, in this order, these subjects: the shots, heard by the listener, which were only target practice; the people who wanted to borrow Riobaldo's guns to shoot a deformed calf they assumed was the Devil; what a real gun fight is like; where the *sertão* might be in relation to where Riobaldo and his listener are (which concludes that the *sertão* is ubiquitous). At first there seems to be a kind of regression, but this sequence (shots, practice, visit, birth of calf) is dissolved when the obsessive theme of the *sertão* appears. Nevertheless, because of the presence of such topics as the Devil, violence, and the *sertão*, it is possible to see the first paragraph as the matrix from which the entire text is derived. The tumult of subjects, the haphazard movement from idea to idea, and the emphasis on the *sertão* as a world of perpetual war also recalls Heraclitian fragment 53, concerning the harmonious discord of nature: "War is the father of all and king of all, and some he shows as gods, others as men; some he makes slaves, others free" (p. 195).

The action of *Grande Sertão* is a series of wars between rival groups of outlaws (*jagunços*). The association of these groups with ideologies is tenuous at best (although one chief, Zé Bebelo, wants to liquidate the *jagunços*) and, for Riobaldo's own development, irrelevant. He is involved, but it is his own inner struggle which most concerns him (and us), an inner struggle like that of Jason in the *Argonautica*, not like Isabel Archer's in *Portrait of a Lady*. The culminating battle in the text, motivated by revenge, takes place with Riobaldo offstage. It is in a sense merely another element in his self-revelation and not a culmination. The idea of culmination or ending is avoided in *Grande Sertão*, and the most significant events occur when they are least expected. Again, this is because life is unpredictable, and despite the moral implications of Riobaldo's concern about belonging either to God or to the Devil, the universe at war is neither good nor evil. In fact, Riobaldo's moral dilemma—he does not know whether or not he sells his soul to the Devil—is subsumed into the greater statement made by the text concerning the world as flux.

The *sertão* is the place where opposites coexist, and Riobaldo's life is progressively revealed to be a metaphor for the *sertão*, just as it is a metaphor for him. But existing in close conjunction with Riobaldo are other characters, the mute *jagunços*, their chiefs, and Diadorim, the most important figure in Riobaldo's life. Guimarães tantalizes the reader with the antinomian idea that a woman, Diadorim, could disguise herself as a *jagunço*, fight, and not be recognized. Here again we see Guimarães using romance fixtures to make his text strange and alien. The subject of Diadorim's masquerade is never raised and, despite some similarities, she is not the amazon or warrior maiden of Ariosto or Calderón. She is a symbol of unsuccessful harmony, a violation of a natural state of affairs. She is a renunciation of the individual's search for his own image, because she has fixed her identity by attempting to define herself as what she is not.

Diadorim's role in Riobaldo's life is that of a catalyst. When she first appears, she is the mysterious "boy" ("o menino," of pp. 80–86/84–91) who involves Riobaldo in a curious rite of passage. Riobaldo is made to cross the São Francisco River in a canoe, a frightening experience. On the other bank he sees the "boy," who urged him to make the crossing, stab a man who suggests that she and Riobaldo are homosexuals. Riobaldo and Diadorim then recross the river. Either something or nothing has happened, but Riobaldo makes no real explanations, simply noting, "I didn't feel anything. Only a transformation I could sense. Lots of important things have no name" (p. 86/91). Riobaldo learns he can be brave, the first step in learning he is not limited in any way. Later he assumes he has reached his limits, but only because he cannot see that he has passed them: "I cross through things—and in the middle of the crossing I don't see!" (p. 30/27). Passage or crossing (the last word of the text is the single word *travessia* accompanied by the symbol for infinity) is reality in *Grande Sertão:* it is an error to invent, as Diadorim does, impassable boundaries.

The relationship between Riobaldo and Diadorim is deceiving. While they seem to constitute an opposition (one darkness, one light) they are in fact mirror twins. Riobaldo and Diadorim are versions of human life itself, one with self-imposed limits, one without; and this is reflected in their biographies. Riobaldo is a bastard who flees when he learns that his godfather and patron, Selorico Mendes, is his father (p. 95/102), as if to deny any but an autochthonous origin. Diadorim, like Camilla, never knew her mother and identified so strongly with her father, Joca Ramiro, that avenging his death became her only reason for living. Diadorim's lust for revenge is like the wrath of Achilles: it shapes the drama of the text, but it does not constitute its total significance.

Riobaldo's ambivalent attitude toward Diadorim is the result of his loving her sexually and hating himself for what he thinks is unnatural. The actual source of disharmony is Diadorim's fixity, her all-consuming passion for revenge, which blinds her to her responsibilities to herself. Her ancestor worship is no virtue in the *sertão*. But of course there is some ambiguity in this. Human life in the text leads inexorably to death; there is no deviation from that pattern. However, human perception of time and the transformation of that interpretation into history is another matter. Diadorim's attempt to "correct" the past is a failure, although this failure must be understood in the exemplary context of what the entire book seems to be saying.

That is, within the text's statement about human fulfillment in the universe of flux there is a negative sign, Diadorim, whose fixity and denial of self represent death-in-life.

Augusto de Campos's ingenious deciphering[4] of Diadorim's name, his pointing out that the letter *d* is a sign both of God ("Deus") and the Devil, is aimed at demonstrating Diadorim's fundamental ambiguity. It would seem however that more than being ambiguous, Diadorim is a negation, negation of sex, negation of self (ancestor worship), and negation of life. We must recall in passing that God is, in the Heraclitian sense, the *logos* or order of the universe; the Devil is His manifestation in the world of phenomena. Riobaldo tells this to the reader without knowing it himself; but he is, after all, a narrator, not an interpreter.

Why it should be Diadorim who initiates Riobaldo into the world of change and violence is a difficult problem. In her role as the boy, Diadorim reveals to Riobaldo the infinite possibilities latent within him, and later it is Diadorim who introduces Riobaldo to the life of the *jagunços*, teaching him how to maintain his individuality and self-respect. Diadorim's function is like that of Virgil in the *Divine Comedy*; she reveals paths she herself cannot take. She must be discarded if Riobaldo is to discover his true mode of being, but this is not easily done because memory, the vast pool out of which Riobaldo draws his narrative, lets nothing die.

The relationship between the individual and his past, between the individual and his progenitors, is ambiguous in *Grande Sertão*. Clearly, Diadorim exaggerates her fealty to her father, and the text seems to say that the dead, locked in the immobility of death, can have no claim on the living, no claim except memory. What an individual should do, either symbolically or literally, is what the character Medeiro Vaz does when he becomes an outlaw:

> he got rid of everything; he divested himself of what he
> owned in land and cattle; he shed everything as if he wanted
> to return to what he was when he was born. He had no
> dependents, no heirs. At the end, with his own hands he set
> fire to the ranch house, the ranch house which had belonged
> to his father, his grandfather, his great-grandfather, and
> waited until it was ashes. Today that place is all overgrown.

Finally he went to where his mother was buried, a little
cemetary at the edge of the pasture; then he knocked down
the fence, pushed over the stones. Soon he felt better; nobody
could find, to stir up with dishonor, the place where his family's bones could be found. (Pp. 36–37/35)

This is more than a romantic gesture, more than an existentialist
belittling of objects and relationships in order to exalt the individual. Medeiro Vaz embraces the *logos* and is reborn.

Guimarães restores the myth of a world where people may
retain their dignity in the face of the unknown, a world not
necessarily of heroes and *jagunços* but of ordinary individuals
who are told their lives are determined by economic and political
forces beyond their control. This is not to say that *Grande Sertão*
is a reactionary text; to the contrary, it demonstrates that the
Medusa of depair is not a genuine threat to those who realize
that history, like all fictions, is what they make of it, not what it
makes of them. In this sense, Guimarães and Cortázar coincide:
they both want to change the reader's life. Cortázar informs us
that we are threatened by routines which rob us of identity; and
Guimarães, echoing Heraclitus, simply points out the folly of
believing in the reality of anything which is essentially a
metaphor.

In "Tlön, Uqbar, Orbis Tertius," Borges describes a situation
in which a fiction, a world made of words, becomes reality; and
this is exactly the kind of fiction, one which stifles life instead of
nurturing it, against which Guimarães fights. To take a version
of reality as reality is to abdicate part of one's individuality. It is
impossible not to bear the yoke of any order, any fiction; but
absolute faith in anything but one's power to change fictions is
an error. In *Cien años de soledad,* García Márquez sets out to
demythologize a national history so that everyone may return to
a *tabula rasa* and find better fictions. The difference between *Cien
años* and *Grande Sertão* is between a text which is an image of an
inexhaustible universe and one which is aimed at proving the
unreality of a particular world. One twists its plot, as it twists
language itself, into the figure eight of infinity; the other draws
the line of linear history back on itself in a circle in order to end
it.

9

Gabriel Garcia
Márquez
A Commodius Vicus
of Recirculation

Eschatology, the principal subject of meditation in García Márquez's *Cien años de soledad* (1967), is alien to Guimarães's text.
The world at war in *Grande Sertão* will always be so, and it is
important that this strife be understood as harmony. In *Cien
años*, the universe is altogether too orderly, because our means
of comprehending it, history, has become the perverted tool of
those interested in forcing time into endless repetition. History
as it stands is a lie for García Márquez, and the business of his
fiction is to seize control of it and bring it to a grim but necessary
conclusion.

Early in *Grande Sertão*, Riobaldo tells a story to which he gives
a false ending, what he calls a "continuação inventada" (p. 67/
70). He observes, as he discusses the lie, that in real life things
do not possess the organic unity found in fictions: "In real life,
things finish with less formality, they don't even finish" (p.
67/70). He knows, however, that his audience has no way of
differentiating between truth and lies in his discourse because
his is the only account of events available. What Riobaldo asserts
here is that fictions tend to be totalities, while life is a continuous
flow. Borges would have agreed with that conclusion, as his
preface to *Morel* suggests, and we would also have to agree that
one of the artificial aspects of art is its unity. The difference
between Borges's precept and *Grande Sertão* lies in the fact that
the latter is a fiction about discord and disorder. It is metonymic

78

in its *mise en scène* and metaphoric in its meaning, so that it is not
at all a disordered text but a text which represents disorder.

Cien años is a metaphor about ideas such as order, fictions, and
endings. It begins and ends bound firmly to its identity as a
book, an enclosed, limited "place," a process begun at one extreme and concluded at the other. It is therefore no surprise that
the final phase of the narrative deals with one of the characters
in the act of deciphering parchments on which is written (in
code) the history of his family and himself. When he finishes
reading, his life ends, as does the text, the book we are reading.
What we have is a text which takes several levels of its own
"textuality" and presents them all simultaneously. As opposed
to Macedonio Fernández's "novela que comienza," a novel that
nʳ er actually begins, *Cien años* is a text which never departs
fully from the concept of ending. The reader holds a book in his
hands which draws ever closer to its end; the last of the principal
characters is reading the story, or history, of his life, which is
drawing to an end: it is all an allegorical exercise about the need
to end fictions.

The reader of *Cien años* is obliged to keep alive in his mind at
all times the idea that the word *fiction* means "feigning or pretending or lying" and, further, to connect those concepts with
the notion that all accounts of events (a class which includes
chronicles and histories) are inevitably fictions. These "givens"
may shed some light on the kind of truth buried in García Márquez's lies. That is, if he is not, because of the nature of the
written word, able to tell us what the truth is, he is at least
capable of telling us one of the categories of discourse in which
truth is, if not absent, at least impotent. *Cien años* holds up the
mirror to fiction—to a very generalized notion of that term—and
sadly concludes that the extraliterary world has been too long
influenced by it and that it must be written out of existence.
Again, this recalls Borges's almost Socratic attitude toward the
danger of taking fictions for realities; here, however, a coun-
terattack is projected.

The layout of *Cien años* reflects its dominant metaphor, endings, which combines both the idea of closure and the ideas of
annihilation and death wish.[1] Just as *Grande Sertão* disorders its

chronology in order to suggest (but not to achieve) total disorder, *Cien años* thwarts progress by telling about events before they happen. The effect of this strategy is to give the reader a "memory" of the textual future. The purpose behind this seems to be the author's desire to reduce time in his book to a kind of present moment in which all events are contemporaneous; that is, he makes into a single moment what is by nature a process which begins and ends. This sounds terribly like Proust's recapture of past events, but its goals are of a different order. Proust deals with the experiences of an individual, bur García Márquez would seem to want to deal with the collective, unconscious memory of all Spanish America. He accomplishes this through a method which may be a parody of Zola's Rougon-Macquart texts, the family history. Where Zola's texts are metaphoric representations of an abstract process, biological inheritance, García Márquez's is in effect a "completed history" of a Spanish American community.

The relationship between these two authors and a concept of history is worth considering. Zola appears to be the heir of Balzac's role as secretary to French history, a history Balzac conceived in dialectical terms. Zola is not interested in that sort of process, but rather paints a picture of "things as they are," by which he means things in decay. That the objects of an era are present in Zola's texts is true, but the value of those things is ultimately moral and not historical. Degeneration is Zola's dominant metaphor, the subject about which he continually writes; and it is perhaps in a renegade naturalist like Huysmans, in a text like *À Rebours*, that we may see this allegory of man's fate represented even more clearly than in Zola. The moral content of these works is divorced from any historical matrix. Like Machado, Zola and Huysmans deal with abstractions dressed in contemporary costume to make their significance real for a particular public.

García Márquez draws a parallel to the Bible when he attempts to define history. An Apocalypse is a revelation of things to come, dramatized to seem present; the biblical wind which blows Macondo, García Márquez's archetypal town, off the map is presented not only as a reality, but also as an event recorded, that is, prophesied, in a book. The history of Macondo, a history of repetition and degeneration, is limited, sentenced by the author, to a one-hundred-year duration and ends with the last words of the text. *Cien años* founds, chronicles, and destroys a world analogous to Faulkner's Yoknapatawpha County with a rapidity that would have astonished the American writer. It would be as though Faulkner, after *Sartoris* (1929), had decided there was a greater need for him to lead his fictional world into destruction than to explore its ramifications. If García Márquez conceives his metaphor-making in a magic sense, as a ritual which will bring about effects in the world, *Cien años* is a death wish for Spanish America.

The beginning of the end begins in the first sentence of *Cien años*: "Many years later, facing the firing squad, Colonel Aureliano Buendía was to remember that remote afternoon in which his father brought him to see ice" (p. 9/11).[2] Before we know it, we are trapped by this virtually meaningless sentence. We have no idea to what present time the "many years later" can refer, nor any understanding of the relationship between that moment and the "remote afternoon" to which it is connected. What is accomplished here is the establishment of a temporal pocket, a span of years between two moments the narrator deems significant and which for the reader are still future events. We are caught in that pocket of years, which gives us two absurd points of demarcation, the effect of which is to insert us *in* a situation. This is not the *in medias res* opening that "ties a knot in time"[3]; this device creates a "now" which balances a before and an after. García Márquez's strategy is to get the reader "in" in a way not dissimilar to Guimarães Rosa's bringing the reader into Riobaldo's "house" for a three day visit.

García Márquez's declarative statement, its matter-of-fact report of data, is what Borges calls classical style in an essay entitled "The Postulation of Reality" (1931).[4] The narrator is not concerned with self-expression or with a personalized utterance of any kind. There is no suggestion that anything extraordinary is occurring or will ever occur. A reality is postulated, not depicted in subjective terms, but simply recorded as if it were normal.

This chronicling of events which may have happened in a future moment, one in which someone remembered something from an unknown past, continues in the second sentence, with one notable difference, "Macondo was at that time a hamlet of twenty bamboo houses built on the bank of a river of diaphanous waters that rushed over a bed of polished stones which were white and huge, like prehistoric eggs" (p. 9/11). A second proper name, Macondo, is introduced without fanfare or explanation. The adverb "entonces" ("at that time") is similarly ambiguous: does it refer to the moment when the colonel is remembering or to the time when he first experienced ice? Obviously the latter, but what possible meaning can this have for the reader, who does not know if the two events are separated by minutes or decades? The final rendering of the imaginary link between the reader and the reality of the text occurs in the metaphor "like prehistoric eggs," which at last tells us that if we continue to believe in the reality of the world in the text, we are fools. It is all a joke, but it is based on a reality which is far from funny. García Márquez will give a plausible chronicle of an imaginary world, which, if we are careless, will blend unnoticed with our own. This has in fact already occurred with other texts, but at least here there are signs to put us on guard.

The first of these is the third sentence, "The world was so recent that many things had no name and to talk about them you had to point at them with your finger" (p. 9/11). If we take this sentence literally, we push the "entonces" of the second sentence back to the dawn of language, to man's Adamic role as namer of things. That it is not that particular point in time to which the narrator refers is made clear later, when there appear references to a suit of armor from the fifteenth century and to the Spanish American colonial era. What does "recent" mean in this context? It seems to refer to a second Eden, to the same intellectual attitude which coined the term "new world," a place where Western man was given a chance to start over. García Márquez tricks the reader into imagining a return to a zero point in time, but simultaneously he points out that there is no moral equivalence between space and time, that a movement into a new space does not erase the legacy men receive from their past, a past which lasts as long as they do.

Escape from what one is, is one of the important motifs of *Cien años*. The pilgrimage or exodus which leads the founders of

Macondo and the Buendía family, José Arcadio Buendía and his
cousin-wife Urusula Iguarán, into the heart of the "new world"
is an attempt to put the past behind, but the heritage of murder
and incest, the signs under which the marriage of the founding
couple is consummated, is inescapable. It is inevitable because
the artist-God of the text has decided it, and the end of the
Buendía family will be an end of a fictional world and, metaphorically, of Spanish American history, which the author includes in his fiction. *Cien años* is a metaphoric maelstrom, an
artistic wish fulfillment of a people's longing for extinction.

Of course, this serious theme, this eschatological atmosphere,
is balanced in *Cien años* by a constant display of humor. In fact,
the very theme of metaphoric or symbolic deaths may be seen as
a prelude to revitalization, and there is certainly a carnival air to
all of the text. At the center of the book (in the tenth of twenty
chapters) there is a real carnival, but where one might have
expected a representation of the world-turned-upside-down of
the kind Bakhtin[5] describes in Rabelais's works, one finds the
reiteration of normalcy, that is, of the arbitrary exercise of power
by the government, that mysterious, anonymous force that per-
petuates the fictions which constitute the nation's history. There
can be no inversion within this text because it is an attempt to set
things right, things already out of order. To affirm its own in-
verted, demonic order, the government intervened in Macondo's carnival in order to assert the primacy of its own inversions.

The combination of the comic and the eschatological in *Cien
años* disconcerts attempts at genre classification, although the
text must, finally, be read as a satire. What complicates the
genre designation is the book's manipulation of a format derived
from romance and mock epic: characters who possess superhu-
man traits, who are archetypes of the human spirit (incarnations
of basic drives; the men are founders, the women maintainers),
and who act in a world where marvels (flying carpets, levitating
priests, unquiet ghosts) are everyday affairs. The blending of
these with a series of actions (civil wars, exploitation by a
banana company) which are completely plausible produces a
situation in which both the marvelous and the banal are made
strange. This is the clearest exercise of the author's combinatory
imagination at work, another example of what Cortázar at-

tempts to lay bare in *Rayuela*. Perhaps this is the most elusive element in *Cien años*, and yet it is at the same time the aspect which most justifies reading it as satire.

The idea of the satirist satirized[6] in his own text sheds a great deal of light on the presence of the character Gabriel in the last phase of the text. This Gabriel, a great-grandson of Gerineldo Márquez, companion of Colonel Aureliano Buendía, shares the view of Macondo's history espoused by the last of the Buendía's, the "true" version, diametrically opposed to the official one. This Márquez is a writer who escapes the destruction of Macondo by going to Paris, where he lives "in the room redolent of boiled cauliflower where Rocamadour was to die" (p. 342/374). Why should the child who dies in the Paris phase of *Rayuela* be mentioned here (as are characters from works by Alejo Carpentier and Carlos Fuentes)? There may be a kind of homage to predecessors in these references, and there may also be another amplification of García Márquez's understanding of his fiction, an expansion to include in the history of Macondo the fictions of other writers like Carpentier, Fuentes, and Cortázar who also see, in *El siglo de las luces*, *La muerte de Artemio Cruz*, and *Los premios*, the falsity of Spanish American history.

Perhaps the inclusion of a portrait of the artist as a young man in the narrative is a means of writing one phase of the author's career out of existence. It would seem difficult to conceive of a sequel to *Cien años*, a return to Macondo after the hurricane. It may well be that the rich flow of literature that runs from *La hojarasca* (1955) to *El coronel no tiene quien le escriba* (1961) and *La mala hora* (1962) had reached its flood tide. The opportunity for a Faulknerian exploration of minds and personalities is not present in García Márquez's work prior to *Cien años* because he does not study psychological types. His archetypes are social (professions or family roles) and political (opposing parties), but not the mad souls we see in Machado de Assis. The manipulation of nonpsychological archetypes may be one more reason for the presence of the author in the text: it may be one more permutation of the death wish, a way of saying "good-by to all that" on an esthetic plane.

The artist here is relegated to a minor role in the action, but his presence is nevertheless linked to the work's overall theme of

endings. In texts to be considered hereafter, *Paradiso* by José
Lezama Lima and *La vida breve* by Juan Carlos Onetti, the artist
will be cast, as he is in *Morel* and *Rayuela*, in a central role. It
should be noted in passing that in all the texts in which an artist
figure is the protagonist, the dominant metaphor of the book
tends to be genesis or production of one kind or another, even if
that production contains or is predicated on a death, while here
the emphasis is on closure.

The plot of *Cien años* is rudimentary, complicated only by the
reiteration of names (a parody perhaps of the Russian novel)
and the proliferation of incidents. Like that of *Rayuela*, it is a
ritual plot, one in which events are not linked by causality but by
a preordained concept of totality, one stated here in the title. No
coincidence therefore is too farfetched, and there is no way to
know why one event should receive more attention than
another. More events could have been interpolated or some removed; the only limitations on the author are those he imposes
on himself. He demonstrates his sense of economy by keeping
virtually all of the action in Macondo, mostly in the Buendía
house, never following his characters out into the world and
leaving those incidents in the form of anecdotes. This strange
adaptation of unity of place gives the illusion of order and reminds the reader that here again he is in a house (or book), a
limited space which contains a world.

García Márquez's eschatological propensities may well be the
basis of his sense of fictional order. The *word* does indeed lie at
the beginning of Macondo, the word of the artist as Borges
imagines him in the preface to *Morel*, creating verbal structures
in which nothing unjustified is present. To be sure, there are
elements in *Cien años* whose presence may not seem justified to
some readers, such as the references to texts by other Spanish
American writers, but even these seemingly capricious moments form part of a ritual in which what matters is not so much
the order or relationship of events as their mere presence. This
is the strategy of myth, the technique of putting everything out
in the open with no clear regard for the delicacies of plot or
causality. Even if *Cien años* is ironic myth-making, it follows the
plan of its nonironic models.

The myths concerned with incest, particularly the Oedipus

story, are not injunctions against incest so much as lessons
about the inhuman nature of fate or destiny. Oedipus does not
deliberately set out to kill his father and marry his mother, unless, of course, the myth is taken as an expression of the son's
subconscious desires. Even in this latter interpretation it is the
son's will to be the father, to be his equal in every way, that
motivates the violence. Myths tell us more than we want to
know about the relationships between family members, but they
do so in a veiled way. In *Cien años,* incest is first mentioned as a
taboo because of biological reasons: children born out of inces-
tuous unions have tails. This is clearly the superficial reason,
analogous to the later explanations of incest taboos on the basis
of a weakening of the capacities of the offspring in societies
"beyond" taboos.

The problem of incest in *Cien años* is not biological, nor is it in
fact moral: there is an instance in which an aunt and a nephew
fornicate (Amaranta and Aureliano José, pp. 126–27/138–39), but
no children are produced. That is, if the act of committing incest
were significant in itself, then the guilt of having done it would
have caused some sort of crisis in the lives of the characters.
Their relations are more an opportunity for sexual comedy (and
sex is treated humorously throughout *Cien años*) than for any
serious or tragic ends. The final act of incest, between Aureliano
Babilonia and his aunt Amaranta Ursula (p. 335/347) is not a cause
but an effect.

The plot consisting of an injunction, a violation, and a retribution (the Fall) is not repeated in *Cien años.* The final incest, which
does produce the child with the tail, is foretold in the parchments Aureliano Babilonia is in the process of deciphering. The
incest, like that of Oedipus, was the result of a predetermined
plan, not an act of will. The question is, why begin and end the
history of Macondo with an act of incest? The answer may lie in
the relationship between repetition and difference. In a world,
and García Márquez seems to envision the world he represents
in this way, in which repetition is the only mode of being, life
cannot develop because it has no place to grow. A concept of
history which states that individuals are born into certain roles
and must spend their earthly existences attempting to har-
monize their lives with the ideal representation of that role al-

lows no room for evolution. True difference can occur only when heterogeneous elements are brought into contact and allowed to generate new forms. This is in fact the essence of the historical world-view behind the novel as a genre.

The essential problem in *Cien años*, structurally and in its attitude toward history, is duration. How long can repetition, even if some measure of degeneration is allowed, take place? The narrator describes how the perpetual "other woman" of *Cien años*, Pilar Ternera, understands the history of the Buendía family in this way: "the history of the family was a meshing of irreparable repetitions, a spinning wheel that would have gone on turning until eternity if it hadn't been for the progressive wearing away of the axle" (p. 334/364). But if the narrator admits the existence of disintegration and fatigue in his system, he nevertheless does not identify to what elements in the family his metaphors of wheel and axle correspond. If we assume them to be one fixed element in constant friction with one moving element, then we may identify them with the feminine and masculine elements in the text: the men tend to be wanderers, the women bound to the house. But unless we enter into numerological interpretations of the number one hundred from the title or of the twenty chapters, we come no closer to the rationale behind the number of steps in the process which leads from the first to the last act of incest.

García Márquez never abandons his Prospero-like role in the orchestration of *Cien años*. His action, as ironic magus, is to appropriate myths, the plot of romance, and things as they are in a Spanish American country and bend them to show his personal vision. His text is charged with comedy, but his irony is bitter, and the last pages of the book are breathtaking in their haste to wipe Macondo away. García Márquez's world, for all its energy, is sterile, dead, alive only as long as the reader turns its pages. The life he describes may exist outside of a book, but it belongs, he seems to be saying, inside the one he creates in order to make cause become effect and reality illusion.

10

Juan Rulfo
The Secular Myth

Another text which uses myth ironically is *Pedro Páramo* (1955) by Juan Rulfo. From the title, the name of the character who is the center of gravity of the world within the text, the reader is obliged to derive a very Eliot-like combination of "stone" (Pedro) and "wasteland" (páramo), and this lugubrious combination would seem to be the author's metaphor for the world he represents. Unlike the world of García Márquez, one which its creator is attempting to bring to an end, the world of *Pedro Páramo* is already dead, deprived of fertility by its eponymous residing genius. Since it is a dead world and yet one which exists within a living cosmos as a kind of dead-end purgatory or limbo, it is a confusion of temporalities, a zone in which the utterances, memories, and thoughts of the dead all ring out simultaneously.

It is for this reason that the reader may find himself at first confused. What seems like a narration by a speaker about to tell his story is in fact a piece of a story told by one of the book's many voices, one of Pedro Páramo's illegitimate sons, Juan Preciado. Chronology here is of little consequence; the book, like a collection of myths, simply tries to put its statement on display. To be sure, within the various episodes chronological order is respected, but the juxtaposition of episode to episode makes the whole incomprehensible as a process and coherent only as a totality. That is, the same sort of "spatialization" of narrative described by Joseph Frank,[1] operative in *Rayuela* and *Tres tristes tigres*, functions here as well. The arrangement is metonymic, but the result is a metaphor, a portrait of a dead land, entrusted by a perverse God to a malignant Peter.

Unlike García Márquez, who places the blame for the perverted status of things on the creation and propagation of fictions which deform reality, Rulfo lays the responsibility for the condition of the world in his text on the egoism of Pedro Páramo himself. Pedro Páramo's role in his cosmos is that of a king in any mythic system. Like Theseus, he is the symbol of power, the highest point on the social pyramid, the controller of the fertility of his world. Comala, the hamlet to which Juan Preciado comes at the false outset of the narrative, is the center of that world and has become a cemetery set in a desert because of Pedro Páramo's curse. That curse, like the retribution experienced by transgressors in myth, is undeserved and irrational. Pedro Páramo decides to destroy Comala because it does not mourn the death of his wife, Susana San Juan, even though it does not know she is dead. Pedro Páramo sees the people enjoying themselves and states, "I shall fold my arms and Comala shall die of hunger." To which the narrator adds, with biblical terseness, "And thus he did it" (p. 143/115).[2]

The text does not explain or describe how Pedro Páramo translates his will into physical reality, because it is not concerned with plastic reality but the moral and metaphysical results of the *cacique*'s rule. Even history, meaning historical events, is inferior to Pedro Páramo's ego: he controls the Mexican Revolution, insofar as it reaches his territory, by sending his own agent to fight in it. The outside world is kept at a distance from Comala, and the only real changes in its order occur when Pedro Páramo ascends to power and when he decides to throttle his domain. There is a curious interaction here between destiny and the individual king figure, because while the social order seems to be eternal and static, one individual can in fact halt the entire system. No one takes Pedro Páramo's place, and the rural world of Comala dries out and dies.

This is precisely the ironic aspect of Rulfo's manipulation of a mythic order, what makes his text a satire and not a romance. Where one might expect a liberator or renewer of society, a new king, one finds only death. The dead voices of the text await

their rest, and we may expect that they will never find it. The
format of romance is again twisted and made strange, as it is in
Cien años, and once more the result is a satiric condemnation of
the world as it is. Rulfo's short but dense novella-length text
shows a world come to an ending without an end, a world in
which not even the dead are allowed to pass into oblivion.

Juan Preciado, through whose eyes we see Comala when the
text opens, has come to claim his inheritance from his father; it is
his mother's last wish, but neither he nor she realizes that
everyone in Comala is somehow Pedro Páramo's bastard. The
inheritance therefore is death (we only realize later that all of
Juan Preciado's speeches are made to a woman, Dorotea, with
whom he shares a coffin), the death in art of a world condemned
by its gods. Even the representative of the deity, the priest Ren-
tería, is overwhelmed by the death wish of the "father" of his
society, Pedro Páramo. There is no possible expiation, resurrection, or escape.

Both *Cien años* and *Pedro Páramo* express despair and a longing
for extinction, and both resort to the supernatural to represent
these concepts. It is as though in order to touch on these ideas
the authors were obliged to turn away from a stage on which
only the plausible could occur, as though what they had to say
were too terrible to be said plainly. This may be why they had
recourse to mythic structures and why, even though he seems to
be depicting a world in realistic terms, Manuel Puig too must
allow some elements of myth to enter into his two studies of
rural Argentina, *La traición de Rita Hayworth* and *Boquitas
pintadas.*

Manuel Puig
Things as They Are

The myth which appears in Manuel Puig's first two texts is that of Uranus-Cronus, the devouring father who is ultimately murdered by his own offspring. In its original form, the myth cycle denotes the struggle between stability and permanence, between the flow of time and its transformation into the circle of repetition. Puig divides his characters into two groups: the larger is that of the repeaters, those whose being is consumed in the reiteration of certain roles (both social and emotional); and the smaller, those who refuse to reenact the parts for which they were seemingly cast by fate. As in the original series of myths, even the exception becomes a regularly repeated process, so that it is impossible to say that the exception is just that, or that he too is a repeater. The world Puig depicts in *La traición de Rita Hayworth* (1967) and *Boquitas pintadas, folletín* (1969) is the world of repetition, where change is superficial and time never translates itself into the dialectical pattern characteristic of the world view that engenders the novel.

It is for this reason, aside from his conception of character, that Puig's works are satires. He, like García Márquez, makes us see that the reality of which the text is a metaphor is itself a falsification, that the only reality present in that world is derived from fictions, from movies, soap operas, and popular music. These created realities are "more real" than everyday life for the people who enjoy them because they are ultimately linked to the great world outside rural Argentina. They are "great passions"

presented in such a way that they acquire meaning and significance beyond the blurred routine of small-town life. Reality
must be "somewhere else" for Puig's characters because
Coronel Vallejos, the setting of both books, is merely a satellite
of Buenos Aires, itself a copy of larger worlds, the world created
by Hollywood, the world of cheap literature, with its wars and
romances, and the world of popular music, where male and
female relationships are expressed as grand archetypes.

It is quite possible that the artificiality of the world depicted in
these two books is a metaphor for Argentina, for all colonial
states, and this would help to explain once again why the
novel's representation of an extratextual world could not occur
in Latin America. For communities condemned to be spectators
in history, reality is somewhere else, in the metropolitan centers
whose reflection they are. García Márquez' *Cien años* attempts to
put the colonial world "out of its misery" by annihilating it. Less
interested in depicting things as they might be, and concerned
with things as they are, Puig does not resort to make-believe.
His characters are all too plausible, as real as the characters in
the melodramatic films of the 1930s and 40s, characters whose
reality, of course, is two dimensional.

Outwardly, it would seem that Puig represents a return to the
naturalist *tranche de vie*, but this is not so. Where the naturalists
use characters to represent the processes they see operating behind human life, Puig attaches the lives of his figures to no such
unified plot or progression. His lives simply unfold over days
and years until they run their meaningless course. Only one
character in either of these two texts possesses a life imbued
with a kind of organic growth, Toto from *La traición*, who stands
for a coming-to-self-awareness of the kind which may represent
the origin of the artist. But we do not witness this transformation, only the possibility of its occurrence.

To see just what Puig does with his characters it is necessary
to see how he arranges events in time, what his concept of plot
is. To this end it might be useful to consider a statement by
Aristotle about the unity a plot (any plot, although he is particularly concerned with dramatic plots) ought to have:

> A poetic imitation, then, ought to be unified in the same way
> as a single imitation in any other mimetic field, by having a

single object: since the plot is an imitation of an action, the
latter ought to be both unified and complete, and the compo-
nent events ought to be so firmly compacted that if any one of
them is shifted to another place, or removed, the whole is
loosened up and dislocated; for an element whose addition or
subtraction makes no perceptible extra difference is not really
a part of the whole.[1]

The quotation comes ironically to the point here because Puig
begins *La traición* in 1933 and ends it in the same year. The final
chapter, a never-sent letter composed at the same time as the
events related in chapter 2, returns the reader to the beginning. Is
this final chapter then, in Aristotle's sense, "not really a part of
the whole," or does the deliberate misplacing of the letter mean
that Puig's text obeys a sense of order alien to Aristotle? From an
Aristotelian point of view, *La traición* has no plot because it has
no action. And yet the text does "hang together," if only because the reader forges the links of causality Puig studiously
omits.

The reader is thrust into the privileged position of omni-
science in *La traición*, just as he is in certain other texts which
superficially resemble Puig's work (*Our Town, Winesburg, Ohio,
Under Milk Wood*, and *Eyeless in Gaza* are examples), and this
apparent renunciation of authority by the author-narrator reflects his attitude toward the meaning or unity of time. Puig
makes his readers into historians in that he requires them to
make sense out of an agglomeration of incidents. Like the reader
of *The Moonstone*, Puig's reader is a detective of sorts, although
unlike Collins's reader he is surprised by a final chapter which is
virtually a *deus ex machina*. Perhaps Puig is ridiculing our creation of his work by reminding us that it is he who has brought
everything into being, and that if we have reconstructed his text,
we have demonstrated the lack of absolute meaning in any
event, any text, or in time itself.

Just at the moment when the "key" to the situation is given,
when Toto's father, Berto, reveals his relationship with his
brother, whose selfish egoism causes the economic crisis under
which Berto labors in the 1930s, the text ends. The family study,
the ironic version of the Rougon-Macquart saga, is rendered
meaningless by the last chapter. All that remains is the

sadomasochistic residue of all human relationships: the real or imagined blows inflicted on us, we in turn inflict on others. The text is, at one level, a metaphor for that idea, just as, at another level, it is a metaphoric representation of a world without direction or significance, a world devoid of transcendence from which meaning has been excluded. The text, taken as an objective description of things as they are in rural Argentina, is an indictment of the colonial world as Fanon would define it, but the text is not only social criticism. We are frustrated by *La traición* because it eludes our interpretations.

In this sense the text mistreats us in the same way we will ultimately mistreat it when we make our interpretations. We must distinguish between this mistreatment, related to the "traición" or betrayal of the title, and the kind of betrayal which characterizes Cabrera Infante's work. Puig's social relationships are based on the kind found in the tango and in Onetti (see chapter 11), mastery and humiliation. We see just this sort of relationship defined when Toto creates a hallucinatory version of the film *The Great Waltz* in a school essay: "That's the way it is, you love or you don't love, and he [Johann Strauss] realizes, on that dock barely illuminated by smoky torches, that he never succeeded in making her [Carla Donner] love him madly; loving madly means to lose one's head and do anything to be near the loved one" (p. 203/194).[2] In Toto's case, the betrayal or humiliation of Tyrone Power by Rita Hayworth (in *Blood and Sand*) becomes the allegorical representation of his being betrayed by his father. It is that insult which provokes a metamorphosis in Toto: he will no longer imitate the social model represented by his father, but will instead become like his mother.

It would be an exaggeration to isolate Toto from his milieu simply because he is the text's center, He is significant because of what he potentially can become, an artist, but he is still a part of a world of repeated conquests and humiliations. The focal point of all human contact in Puig's two texts is the family, and it is there that the master-victim relationships are formed. It is also no coincidence that the family incarnates time, that it crystalizes the problem of change and differentiation in the midst of repetition. It is therefore to the family that we must turn in order to see just what sort of dominant metaphor, or action in the Aristotelian sense, Puig may be manipulating.

It is in the first chapter of *La traición* and throughout *Boquitas pintadas* that we see the family used as the keystone of Puig's discourse. Chapter 1 of *La traición*, "In the House of Mita's Parents, La Plata, 1933," is mysterious because no characters are identified. They are voices in a room, voices that express their identities by being associated with roles: father, mother, daughter, secretary, shoemaker, "other woman," identities not personalized by the speaker. The reader gradually sorts out the various identities, but what does he have when he finishes? Only words, characters without character, the minor figures of a never-to-be-written Dickensian novel about rural Argentina. The first sentence, pronounced by one of the female figures, defines the world we are about to enter: "The cross stitch made with brown thread on undyed linen, that's why the tablecloth turned out so nice for you" (p. 7/7). There is no meaning here, no transcendent value of any sort; this is a world in which meaning, in the sense of individuality, is a virtually unthinkable, and certainly unspeakable, possibility.

A paradoxical aspect of Puig's families is their inability to function as a unit. The individual lives, despite their lack of individuality, do not cohere. Puig's mode of representation, in which named characters appear in isolation, not interacting before our eyes (although dialogue passages are quoted in the chapters), supports this concept of a fragmented society. Whether the technique gives rise to the concept or whether the technique reflects an actual social situation is difficult to determine. It would seem that the problem is ultimately a false one because the implied distinction between a subjective or objective picture of the world—which would tell us whether Puig's assessment is public or private, valid or not—is not being made in the text itself. *La traición*, like *Boquitas pintadas*, is imbued with irony, and no matter what the actual nature of the world "outside" the text is, Puig's representations suggest that it is a world lacking real community.

The ultimate level of narrative objectivity must be one in which the author not only does not judge his characters but also

treats them as objects. This clinical attitude is not as apparent in
La traición, where there is, strictly speaking, no narrator linking
the individual soliloquies, but is manifest in *Boquitas pintadas*,
where characters are described in much the same way as the
things around them. In a chapter or "installment" composed of
letters, Puig simply inserts this statement between two of them
to report the letter-writer's activity, "She gets up, changes
clothes, checks the money in her wallet, leaves the house, and
walks six blocks to the post office" (p. 18/17).[3] There is a determined effort here to avoid narrative interpretation, and it might
be comparable in some ways to the techniques of Robbe-Grillet.
The difference would arise from Puig's grounding his work in
the recognizable objects of an extraliterary world. Most prominent among these artifacts are, of course, the films, the songs,
and the literary works in which the characters find "real life." It
is therefore a situation in which one set of fictions finds its ideal
or its purified identity in another.

Such mirroring, coupled with the "aimless" character of
Puig's texts, their wax museum–like atmosphere, would seem
simultaneously to demand and preclude connecting the text
with the real world. He certainly holds the mirror up to life, but
how are we to know which is the distorted image? This problem
recalls Borges's injunction, in the preface to *Morel*, against works
of art that imitate life, which are presumably metonymic in nature when they should be metaphoric. Even if we discount
Borges's concept of the difference between realism and
metaphoric writing, even if we see all mimetic forms as ultimately metaphoric, we are left in a quandry with regard to Puig
because we cannot see where either of his texts is "going." They
are both in a sense maps of a peculiar sort, maps which refuse to
identify the locale they represent in great detail.

Their Aristotelian action, their soul, is therefore not a plot but
a condition. Through a process of accumulation and amplification, Puig brings to the reader a few simple ideas. In *La traición*
he is concerned with dominance and submission, repetition and
difference; in *Boquitas pintadas* he creates a display of passions,
together with an ironic meditation on life as a "passion," that is,
as a dying. In this latter text, Puig turns to a popular form, the
serial novel, for a means which will allow him to create figures

totally unrelated to a historical milieu, who would, nevertheless, be recognizable because of language and setting. The serial novel provides the ideal medium because it utilizes relatively short, self-contained chapters which are devoted either to complication or portraiture, to the expansion of the work's control over time (its false, paratactic unity based on an ability to generate a "past"), and its display of characters who are emotions incarnate.

It is a false conclusion, espoused by many, that serial fiction, the serial novel specifically, is intrinsically inferior to other forms. In literature there can be no hierarchies based on genre or on popularity because such valorizations assume a uniform relationship between the genres and society throughout history. Claude Lévi-Strauss, who complains so often about Western civilization's being a slave to history, is remarkably history-bound himself when he meditates on the serial novel and the expanded myth (the episodic narratives which blend stories from many mythic sources). In *L'Origine des Manières de Table*, he notes:

> Nevertheless, it would be a mistake to forget that though the episodic myth and the serial novel cross paths, they follow tracks leading in opposite directions. The serial novel—the final state of degeneration in the novel—meets up with the lowest forms of myth, which are themselves an emergent form of fiction in its first freshness and originality. In its search for a "happy ending," the serial novel finds in the rewarding of the good and the punishing of the wicked a vague equivalent to the closed structure of myth, transposing it on to a caricature map of a moral order through which a society dedicated to history thinks it can replace the logical ordering of nature which it has abandoned (or, possibly, been abandoned by).[4]

For Lévi-Strauss, the novel (although there is no way to know just what he means by that word) is a sign of decline: "it was inevitable that the novel should tell a story that ends unhappily and that it should be, as a genre, in the process of ending unhappily itself" (p. 213). Here is a judgment Puig's texts render absurd. To correlate the decline of a society with a "decline" in its literary forms is to equate the parallel but different lines of

literary and social history. That the novel is born "from the
attenuation of myth," and that it "is reduced to an ever-flagging
pursuit of structure until it reaches a destiny which it can per-
ceive only too clearly, without being able to find either within
itself or outside itself the secret of a pristine freshness" (p. 213) is
to limit the novel to the French novel (although even this seems
to be a grotesque distortion) and to omit, presumably to give a
"happy ending" to the theory at stake, any consideration of
literary history.

And yet, in his blindness Lévi-Strauss illuminates one aspect
of Puig's accomplishment, his galvanizing of certain forms and
his utilization of myth. Lévi-Strauss attempts to explain that the
appearance of a certain form augurs good or ill for a given society, as if the writers were constrained, perhaps by the *Zeitgeist*,
to work within a certain limited area. Puig, like Lévi-Strauss's
own *bricoleur*, utilizes what is immediately available to him, but
he bends it to his own purpose. Why is the serial novel format
used in *Boquitas pintadas*? Why is *La traición* arranged in serial
form? Is Puig's satire also a sign of decline and fall or is it a sign
of life? These are unanswerable questions, just as Lévi-Strauss's
speculations on the historical destiny of genres is a premise he
cannot prove. Certainly we can question Lévi-Strauss's value
judgments and conclude that his idea of myth's "pristine freshness," which he opposes to the "degenerate" serial novel, ig-
nores totally the relationship between individual text and tradition.

Of course, in the case of Puig the question of literary tradition
is confusing. Which is the tradition to which he is to be related,
and which is the tradition to which he relates himself? This is a
crucial matter, because when we say that he is utilizing in
Boquitas pintadas the revitalized form of the serial novel, we are
falling into a trap similar to the one which engulfed Lévi-
Strauss. Just as it is difficult to explain (excluding irony as a
reason) why modern writers so often resort to myth, it is equally
difficult to know why a writer reworks an extant form. For
example, the detective novel or story was not always considered
the appropriate form to be explored by serious writers. Borges
and others have not only changed our ideas about the merit of
such forms, but have also led us to reread the works of the past

in a new light. It may not, therefore, be justifiable to conclude that *Boquitas pintadas* is necessarily an ironic utilization of the serial novel when it may simply be a finer rendition of it.

Don Quijote makes use of elements from the chivalric novel, but it is not itself a chivalric novel. In this Puig shows himself to be working within a form and not in the mode of parody. It is also the case that writers such as Dickens and Machado de Assis wrote serialized fiction (as did so many writers of the nineteenth century), and that for many of the consumers of such literature their writings would have been more interesting versions of what they experienced in their everyday reading. Puig's major limitation was having to publish his text as a book instead of publishing it first in installments as did his predecessors. Except for that difference in tempo, in the rate at which the text is made available to the reader, there is no reason to distinguish Puig's work in *kind* from other serial novels.

Naturally, the *novel* half of the term *serial novel* is not a serious genre designation. Puig is a satirist, and his characters are reduced to emotional or social types. It might have been possible for his work to have been romance, but not with the same *dramatis personae*. Puig concentrates on the audience most likely to read a serial novel as a source for characters, and this is probably his greatest deviation from the traditional serial novel, especially that of the nineteenth century. The author who in France gave his name to the form, Octave Feuillet (1821–90)— the father of the *feuilleton*—supplied his readers (*Camors* is a good example of his work) with a wide spectrum of social types, including a look at the aristocracy. This tendency to show an idealized yet plausible world, the world Emma Bovary found in books, is absent in Puig, except for the films his characters see. But what he sacrifices in glitter he gains in social homogeneity, which makes his work so much like today's televised soap operas.

His characters are from both ends of the middle and lower classes, groups which share institutions—public schools for example—and whose social contact is natural. This enables Puig to present a thorough portrait of class frictions (the character Esther in *La traición* being the best portrait of a Peronist working-class sensibility available) as well as cultural cohesion, one derived from experiencing the same films and the same popular music. At the same time, there is no sense in Puig's works that he is striving to fill in the blank spaces in a social picture of rural life. The reader does not feel the absence of the aristocratic *estanciero* or see the need to incarnate the conflicting ideologies of the upper or lower classes. Like Neruda's "Galope muerto," a simile in which only the comparison is present, but not the object being compared, Puig's texts seem to be metaphors for a society as it is, seen from the perspective of its social relationships, with no overt reference to a class struggle set on a historical plane.

The absence of currents which would polarize the characters in sides of a dialectical conflict makes the reader acutely aware of the energy behind the text, the artist. Unlike Bioy Casares, who shows the creation of the artist, unlike Cortázar, who shows the artist at work, and unlike Juan Carlos Onetti, who synthesizes in *La vida breve* what Bioy and Cortázar do, Puig's invisible artist calls attention to himself by his very absence. He is the final distillation of the nineteenth-century artist-god, everywhere and nowhere, revealing himself through his stylistic dexterity. His detachment also thrusts upon the reader the full weight of interpretation, the esthetic and moral decisions concerned with Puig's representation of life in Coronel Vallejos. The difference between naturalism, for example, and Puig's objectivity is his refusal to impose on the reader a nonesthetic bias. What the reader does with the text is up to him; Puig simply gives him the raw material.

Puig's reduction of the artist-in-the-text to a potentiality (Toto) and his utilization of an impersonal "camera lens" narrator in *Boquitas pintadas* are exceptional cases in the new Latin American narrative. The strongest trend, represented by Bioy Casares, Cortázar, Onetti, Cabrera Infante, and Lezama Lima, is to use the artist, and particularly the artist plying his trade, as the center of the text. This is consistent with a great deal of romantic and postromantic literature, especially the German tradition from Goethe to Mann. The usual explanation for this phenomenon is the alienation of the artist from his society, the loss of his primordial role as extoller and reformer of the social order, and his romantic self-consciousness, which moves him to constant introspection. Whatever the real reasons may be, even assuming the above to be untrue, the simple fact is that a great deal of modern literature is about the artist and the processes of esthetic creation. Even satire, traditionally an externally oriented genre, has become introspective and self-analytical over the last two centuries.

12

Juan Carlos Onetti &
Jose Lezama Lima
A Double Portrait of
the Artist

Juan Carlos Onetti's *La vida breve* (1950) and José Lezama Lima's *Paradiso* (1968) transcend the commonplaces of the *Kunstlerroman* in order to make statements about two specific classes of verbal artist, the prose narrator and the poet. The two books accomplish this by dramatizing the tension between metaphor and metonymy, actually finding in them the symbols or icons to represent the poet and the narrator. *La vida breve* consists of a series of lives lived by one man, each life flowing out of the preceding one, while *Paradiso* contains a life in which each moment is metaphoric, charged with meaning, suggestive of myriad possibilities. That is, the story of the narrator not only is metonymic but might be said to represent metonymy, while the history of the poet is a series of metaphors in apposition.

Even the titles of the two works suggest their orientation. Onetti's title is ironically Hippocratic, even though the text does not in fact compare art with life, dealing instead with lives within a fiction. It further suggests the infinite unfolding of "brief lives" in the author's mind. This author is conceived of in Borgesian terms as a timeless figure made up of all authors, telling one story over and over again in endless permutations. Lezama Lima's text promises to contain references to Dante's third canticle (we should recall in passing that in Spanish *paradise* is *paraíso* and not *paradiso*) in which Dante the poet is granted a glimpse of the godhead. Lezama's text however takes place on earth in a very real (though marvelous) Havana, and it would seem that we are to see Cuba as a kind of paradise of the mind, or at least of the memory. Just as at the end of Dante's *Paradiso* there occurs the moment in which the poet is told to write down what he has experienced, what we have experienced as a text, the end of Lezama's *Paradiso* is the moment when the young poet, José Cemí, comes into his poetic majority. The end in both cases is a beginning, the moment when the text the reader has in his hands becomes possible. In Lezama's book it is also the moment of death, the master-poet Oppiano Licario dies and passes the torch to José Cemí, who may now, like Dante, begin to write.

Paradiso is both a complex and a complicated work (to juxtapose two complementary words Lezama toys with in his "Complejo y complicado" note in *Tratados en La Habana*[1]), complex in the rigor of its intellectual content and complicated in its manner of presenting those ideas. It might be said that the relationship between ideas and realization here resembles the Aristotelian relationship between action and plot—a city is suffering because of a plague (action); the king tries to discover the cause of the plague (plot). To trace, for Lezama, the formation of the poet is not a simple process; he feels obliged to gather together all the elements which might, however vaguely, contribute to the configuration, including, naturally, the more obvious sources: family, friends, and contemporary society.

The first story structure in *Paradiso* is, not surprisingly, the family history, a device he may have copied from Mann's *Buddenbrooks*. He may also have borrowed from Mann's *Tonio Kröger* the conjugation of symbolic poles, north and south, to produce a mixed individual of contradictory tendencies, a metaphor for the artist instead of an explanation of why someone would become an artist. The principal thrust of *Paradiso* is metaphoric; it is not the process of narration taken as an explanatory process that matters but the narrative taken as an entelechy or crystallization. That is, in the poet's life there are myriad episodes—deaths, births, student riots, the entire world of circumstance—but it is the relationship of the poet to his world that seems to be of paramount importance. His world is charged with possibilities, with meanings, with symbols, but all of these magic connections or circuits are available only to him because the poet is somehow

more than human. From the title on, we know we are in a
metaphoric space. Dante's paradise is not in this world, and
what he describes is not even paradise as it is but words about a
metaphor, since paradise as it is would be incomprehensible to
the pilgrim. In Lezama's *Paradiso*, we are given a metaphor, not
an object; not primary experience, but the experience of the
word, the poet's true domain.

The description of the poet's relationship to his father in
Paradiso illustrates this metaphoricity and underlines the difference between a work oriented toward the narration of
progressive actions and narrative taken as the accumulation of
details which constitute a metaphoric totality. In this passage,
the third-person narrator describes the reaction of a friend,
Fronesis, to José Cemí's lineage:

> But Fronesis too was surprised when he met Cemí. He had
> seen just what it was that surrounded him. The strength
> which came to him through his father's line; how the death of
> the colonel [Cemí's father] had become an absence as throb-
> bing and growing as the most immediate presence. This visi-
> bility of absence, this domain of absence was Cemí's
> strongest sign. In him, what was not there, was; the invisible
> occupied the foreground of the visible, becoming something
> visible with vertiginous possibilities; absence was presence,
> penetration, Stoic *ocupatio* [sic]. Absence in him was never
> that Genesis in reverse which has been pointed out in Mal-
> larmé, but to the contrary was as innate as bodies working
> out the proportions of rhythm. (P. 349/328)[2]

We see in this passage a particular technique for arranging narrative. First there is a declaration: Fronesis sees what it is that
surrounds Cemí. This "something" is the "strength which came
to him through his father's line." His father's death had become
an absence so "throbbing and growing" that it is as if the absence were a presence. This absence which is a presence is the
element that most characterizes Cemí. The absence is a presence, the state of being penetrated or possessed (the *ocupatio*
mentioned in the passage), not in the way it is expressed in
Mallarmé, a kind of creation or Genesis in reverse, but similar to
the transformations in a body as it passes through the various
phases of a series of rhythmical movements. The arrangement of

the prose here begins with the postulation of an idea: first the "something" which surrounds Cemí; then there appears an equivalent of that "something," "strength"; then yet another equivalence, "the death of the colonel," which in some way is the equivalent of the colonel or perhaps a synecdoche for him. Then another equivalence is established: the colonel's death is an absence which is like a presence. What we have, then, is a chain of equivalencies: something, the father's strength, his death, which is a presence, being penetrated or possessed, and then back to Cemí.

The entire passage is based on the principle of metaphor, on the substitution of one sign (and Cemí's name is related to the idea of divinity as well as to the notion of the linguistic sign[3]) for another, on the accumulation of signs which in one way or another are equivalent. Perhaps we should recall what Jakobson says in *Fundamentals of Language:*

> The principle of similarity underlies poetry; the metrical parallelism of lines, or the phonic equivalence of rhyming words prompts the question of semantic similarity and contrast; there exist, for instance, grammatical and antigrammatical but never agrammatical rhymes. Prose, on the contrary, is forwarded essentially by contiguity. Thus, for poetry, metaphor, and for prose, metonymy is the line of least resistance, and consequently, the study of poetical tropes is directed chiefly toward metaphor. (Pp. 95–96)

Despite the fact that any narrative structure is a combination of metaphor and metonymy, poetry tends toward metaphor and prose tends toward metonymy. Lezama's text is a metaphor for the poet's life, presented as if it were a poem, in metaphoric fashion. Lezama's prose is simultaneously complex and complicated because it does not aspire to be prose but poetry; it does not proceed or move forward but repeats itself in an accumulation of equivalencies.

In *La vida breve*, we find exactly the opposite procedure. The text is about the formation of a narrator, not in his intellectual formation or his family background, but how he becomes a creating machine. If the method underlying *Paradiso* is the creation of metaphors, the procedure of *La vida breve* is the generation of metonymy, the passing from one element to another, the linking of heterogeneous, not aprioristically linked elements.

Beginning with the title, which is perhaps a metaphor, we see the discontinuous possibilities of *La vida breve:* it might be a reference to Hippocrates' first aphorism, "Ars longa, vita brevis," in its Latin translation; it might be part of a verse sung by the character Mami (chapter 23), or it might be a sexual reference: for the "small death" of orgasm there must be a "short life" which precedes it. It might also be a reference to an opera by Manuel de Falla, *La vida breve*, but the link between sex and death would seem to be the most significant connection. Sexuality in Onetti's works is, like all human relations in his writings, contaminated, another moment of domination, humiliation, or degradation. It is simply a kind of egoism which has little to do with pleasure. There is little eroticism in Onetti's texts, and sexuality is usually linked with violence, with violation or rape, never with love. The role sexuality plays in the lives of Onetti's women may also be seen as a function of a "vida breve": just before sexual maturity the female is pure, almost a spirit, but with sexuality and maturity the ethereal "girl" spirit dies and the woman is born. But it is the man who forges the transition, who idealizes the girl, who "kills" her out of lust, and who discards the tarnished woman.

At the outset, we find the protagonist, Juan María Brausen, waiting for something to happen, something which will give him a new life. As the first chapter unfolds, Brausen is listening to his next-door neighbor, Queca, a prostitute, talking with a man; and as he listens, he postulates bodies around the voices: "I imagined her mouth in motion . . . the thick arms I supposed her to have. . . . The man was probably in shirtsleeves, corpulent and jowled" (pp. 11–12/3).[4] These elements do not as yet constitute a metaphoric equivalent for the reality on the other side of the wall; they are instead possible continuations or developments for those possibilities. This first scene recalls Julio Cortázar's novella *Las babas del diablo*,[5] in which we find a man who exists as a bridge between worlds. He is Franco-Chilean, a translator, and a photographer. One day he sees what he imagines to be a seduction in progress, decides to intervene, and does so by photographing the couple in question. Later he develops and enlarges his photo, continuing to interpret it. Suddenly he loses his status as a human being and becomes a spirit capable of using a typewriter, but condemned to be a camera lens. The protagonist in this tale is a metaphor for the artist who re-creates what chance gives him and who is, in turn, condemned to lose his own identity in order to become his own creation, a case similar to *Morel*.

Cortázar's story provides a good contrast to Onetti's text because it uses roughly the same materials for different ends. What interests Onetti is the process of creating a narrative, while Cortázar is interested in the result of such creation. A tendency to metaphor in Cortázar creates the need for a metaphoric, binary protagonist, a man with dual citizenship and two languages. On the other hand, Brausen is not a figure in himself of any such allegorical value; he is a narrative function. His activity consists not so much in representing but in connecting elements. His is not so much a portrait of the artist, but of a man who becomes an artist by trying to transform his own life, by trying to dream a new life.

If we consider chapter 15, "Small Death and Resurrection," we find a summary of Brausen's condition, along with the narrative technique that reflects such a condition. In this chapter, Brausen and his wife Gertrudis are in their apartment, but there are, in a sense, other people present. In an earlier chapter (12), Brausen creates another identity, Arce, and in that guise has sexual relations with Queca. As he is having those relations, he imagines himself to be one of the characters he is creating for a film script, Dr. Díaz Grey. He is at the same time Brausen acting the part of Arce, who is having sexual relations with Queca, while imagining he is Díaz Grey, who is having sexual relations with another character, Elena Sala. Aware of possessing three distinct identities, Brausen remarks:

> I embraced her, sure that nothing was happening, that all of it was nothing more than one of those stories I would tell myself every night to help myself to fall asleep; I was sure I wasn't myself but Díaz Grey; he was the one embracing a woman, the arms, the shoulder, and the breasts of Elena Sala, in his examination room, at midday, finally. (P. 107/78)

At this stage in his dreaming, Brausen must maintain all his identities intact. Despite the fact that he, as Arce, believes him-

self to be Díaz Grey, he feels linked to Arce because Arce is
beaten by a pimp (Ernesto) in another chapter. Brausen is committed to Arce because of violence, as we see in chapter 15,
where Brausen muses over the revolver which will protect him
in his next fight with Ernesto, the revolver that is also an affirmation of sexual potency. Violence engenders consciousness,
the awareness of hierarchies, but violence also is a prelude to
death, the sacrifice of one life to affirm the existence of another.
Eroticism in Onetti, as it is in Georges Bataille,[6] is a means to
achieve continuity, a prolongation of life through the sacrifice of
another. Brausen's initial disgust with his life is caused by the
fall of Gertrudis into contaminated womanhood. Arce and Díaz
Grey are born out of the sacrifice of Gertrudis, but even in these
new lives the same pattern is maintained: someone (a woman,
generally) must be sacrificed to begin the new life, and someone
must continually be sacrificed (the girl, the pure spirit, must be
sullied, turned into the woman, and rejected) in order to insure
prolongation, to fight against discontinuity.

Later in chapter 15, Brausen imagines his lineage, an infinite
line of Brausens, and he imagines himself dead: "I here, dead,
momentary culmination of a theory of dead Brausens ... impersonal prologues to carrion ..." (p. 131/96). He imagines
himself living just so he may die, "to rehearse my death and
discreetly observe its face; in order to be stretched out and in
peace in this night, suppressing myself, being myself, after all,
in the annihilation, when the silence of this woman spreads over
my precarious beatitude, this woman who stared with desirious
and conventional nostalgia at the last reddish light of my false
last day ... " (p. 131/96). Gertrudis's metaphoric death enables
Brausen to imagine his own death and resurrection: he becomes,
under her eyes, a kind of Christ figure (he even repeats the
words "stabat mater"). His death is merely the transition to a
new life, a resurrection, while she is condemned to dwell in the
half-life of memories, of the "brief life" she possessed before her
fall. Many traditions are reduced to ash by the irony of the
scene: the amatory tradition out of which Dante's *Vita nuova* (a
new life born out of love) emerged, the whole idea of ritual
death and resurrection, whether spiritual or physical, related to
erotic love or to religion; all of these are rendered ridiculous in

Onetti's satire, where the only object of value is the narrative itself.

Onetti's protagonist sees himself as a unit in a series, a series of figures more or less identical to him. Even the lives he creates as alternatives (metaphors which become metonymies) are variations on his own life, where relationships between men and women are still based on domination and humiliation. Instead of a return to the beginning at the end of the text, as we find in *Paradiso*, where satire is again at the service of esthetics, we see at the end of *La vida breve* the continuation of all that has occurred. Instead of Brausen, we are now with Díaz Grey, but this change of character signals no change of meaning or direction; the plot goes on. If *Paradiso* closes the circle of metaphor as closely as possible at the end by bringing the objects to be substituted into approximation, *La vida breve* continues to proliferate as it closes, opening the way for more and more "brief lives."

13

José Donoso
Endgame

Both in their titles and in their *mis en scène*, *La vida breve* and *Paradiso* demonstrate that the *locus* of writing is language, literary language, and that all "new" texts are reflections and echoes of extant models. The writing of a narrative is an exercise in interpolation: just as a narrative "opens" to allow the insertion of an interpolated tale, just as the narrator of *Morel* enters Morel's film, the literary tradition constantly opens to allow variation. But all variation, all novelty, is perforce limited. Recombination may be infinite, but the elements recombined inevitably show family traits. This sense of literature as a "family affair" may go far as a metaphor useful for understanding Latin American narrative, a literature which, as we have seen, often chooses as its framework the history of families or of familial combinations such as brothers or doubles. Throughout the texts under consideration here there is the idea of repetition and variation, of text-begetting-text, of family rivalry, of incest, and of persistence through time: survival. Like many of Beckett's narrators, like vast families of orphans, these works all try to reach a goal, a point, yet they are at the same time reluctant to reach it because of the ominous connotations of closure. The family, the text, is born to die, to be unable to "go on," but to be incapable of anything else.

This paradoxical will-to-survive coupled with a will-to-conclude draws attention once again to the linguistic aspects of the literary text. The forces of metaphor and metonymy, manifest in Bioy Casares, Sarduy, Lezama, and Onetti—but just as clearly present in Cortázar and Puig, whose texts oscillate between alternative endings or return to the beginning at the end—have a symbiotic yet antagonistic relationship. Metonymy is oriented toward keeping things moving, while metaphor is oriented toward finality, just as the instinct of self-preservation is in obvious conflict with the idea of suicide. Narrative may indeed be said to resemble the ego in the id-ego-superego configuration. Instead, however, of being a monolithic totality, it is made up of conflicting elements which may ultimately fall out of harmony and into chaos. A text's "natural death" occurs when its final metaphor is forged, when the only possible prolongation would be verbatim repetition.

The concept of plot is the reduction of these oppositions to a deceptively harmonic concept of order: a beginning automatically postulates an end; a middle represents the holding in abeyance of these two poles, the illusory time in which both are repressed. The fragmentary or fragmented text, *Tres tristes tigres* or *Rayuela*, for example, raises that act of repression to its highest point. In the same way, a sung epic would suppress the whole (the entire song) in order to concentrate on the scene, and it would create thereby the illusion of a text without boundaries. The poignancy of Gertrude Stein's "rose is a rose is a rose" or Beckett's "Ping" is that the moment the first printed word is reflected by the reader's eyes, the text enters into combat with itself: how long can it keep going before it swallows itself up in its own metaphor?

It is precisely this idea of metaphor versus metonymy, of continuance versus closure, that is enacted in José Donoso's *El obsceno pájaro de la noche* (1974). The narrative is concerned in this case with itself, with keeping itself moving, keeping alive despite its own tendency to end. Donoso's text, for our purposes, combines elements from Sarduy, Onetti, and Lezama: the idea that the characters are nothing more than permutations of the poles of narrative, metaphor and metonymy, the idea that these poles are in opposition, and the idea that the only possible subject of the narrative is the narrative itself, that the text is a self-consuming, self-generating verbal object.

Such a text is, of course, monstrous, but we should recall that

the Latin American texts examined in this essay are all monstrous in their way. Monstrosity is an essential part of satire,
monstrosity understood as an exaggeration of any kind which
renders the distorted object grotesque. But this distortion tran-
scends the comic, the parodic, and the satiric (in the sense of
that which pokes fun at something else) because it erases the
relationship between the real (the normal) and the grotesque
(the distorted version of the real). Satire, as we have been ob-
serving it, seems to be saying, "You may see or be tempted to
see a relationship between the real and the unreal here, but you
must forget that relationship, forget the idea of mimesis or representation." Satire may have begun as vituperation and may
have been used as a moralizing tool, but these are not its limits:
satire is the drama of idea in conflict with idea, of Coleridgean
fancy freed from the ordering constraints of imagination. Like
the reality of dreams, satire utilizes elements similar to things in
the "real" world but organized in a form, a language, different
from that of reality. To see satire exclusively in terms of carnival
inversions or as a means whereby we see behind everyday reality is to simplify it, reduce it. Perhaps this is our only means of
controlling a potentially destructive, antisocial force: satire, as
Petronius, Quevedo, and Swift practice it, is one step from
madness, from the devaluation of all our fictions of order, *misura*,
and reason.

It is not unthinkable that the author of a monstrous text might
himself be a monster—it is difficult to find readers who think
Céline, for example, is anything other than a fiend. Wayne
Booth's moralistic statement about Céline might stand as a
judgment on all satirists: "Though Céline has attempted the
traditional excuse—remember, it is my character speaking and
not I—we cannot excuse him for writing a book which, if taken
seriously by the reader, must corrupt him."[1] Booth, writing in a
tradition of literary criticism that runs from Arnold to Plato, is
certain that he knows what is moral, what corrupts, what
should and should not be allowed to be printed. He also assumes that the reader of Céline will read only Céline, that he
will be swept away by Céline. This surely flies in the face of the
entire literary tradition, particularly that part which sees the
artist as a kind of outlaw, the kind of author Cervantes imagined

in Ginés de Pasamonte or Shakespeare in Autolycus. A. Bartlett Giamatti[2] has carefully delineated this figure in Renaissance literature as that of Proteus, and Proteus is certainly the name one would be inclined to ascribe to the satirist, who, as verbal *magus*, weaves a labyrinth of words to make us aware of the horror of order, the very order consecrated by the divinely inspired *vates*. That the satirist's vision is ironic or dark is certainly often true; but without darkness, light is insignificant or blinding.

Proteus, the demonic element in language, its powers to seduce, to fool, is at the center of *El obsceno pájaro de la noche*, where once again art, artist, and text are fused. The ironic Arcadia of literature Borges figures forth in so many of his texts, and explicitly describes in "Borges and I," is one in which the immortality conferred by the text changes the author into an involuntary Proteus, changed in meaning by every reader who takes up the book. This proliferation of shape-shifters may seem dizzying, yet it helps to define the status of the literary text, particularly the satire, because it points out the fundamental ambiguity of any verbal work of art—the loss of significance that occurs when the text leaves the author's hand, mixed paradoxically with the text's apparent possession of meaning. Donoso depicts in his satire the literary work of art in action, a grotesque work-in-progress that fights to stay alive as it seeks to destroy itself.

In addition to Proteus, two other literary metaphors may serve as aids to reflection on *El obsceno pájaro de la noche*, the Ptolomaic cosmology and Mary Shelley's Dr. Frankenstein. The Ptolomaic cosmology, as Dante used it, saw the universe as a series of concentric spheres: to this world-within-world concept Donoso adds, in the cosmology of his text, the ideas of the microcosm and reversibility. The idea of the microcosm, related to synecdoche, suggests that the fragment constitutes a minute recapitulation of the whole. (In the Renaissance, man was often spoken of as a microcosm because he seemed to be the entire universe in miniature.) *El obsceno pájaro de la noche* is composed of successive story layers (as is *La vida breve*), each one a version or metaphor of the next, an arrangement which suggests that the reader will eventually reach a center that will give him a perspective on the rest, a vantage point from which the relationship of all the parts may be seen. But this idea is replaced by that of reversibility, the idea that the peeling off of the successive layers brings the reader no closer to the center and that at a certain point the process reverses itself. Instead of getting to the center, the reader finds himself again at the beginning.

The Ptolomaic system is repeated throughout the text by the idea of enclosure. The first scene of the book takes place in the Casa de Ejercicios Espirituales de la Encarnación de la Chimba, a combination convent and old-age asylum. The old women in the convent are continuously putting things into packages, tucking the packages away, just as they themselves have been tucked away in the cloister, just as a dead body is put inside a coffin, as bad memories are repressed. The pattern established here makes all acts of enclosure—the sexual act, the gestation of a baby, wearing clothes, binding a text within covers—metaphors for each other. The narrator, who speaks to us from within various *personae* or masks, encloses himself within various identities, each one breeding another: the book encloses the pages, the words are enclosures we fill with meaning, the totality is enclosed within an interpretation. The closer we come to the text the further away from us it moves; at best we can see the layers as the narrative's own desperate attempt to create the illusion of infinite space, to keep on moving despite the fact that it is doomed, limited by its own nature, that of any book.

The kind of artist-creator depicted in Mary Shelley's *Frankenstein, or The Modern Prometheus* (1816) prefigures in many ways the narrator in *El obsceno pájaro de la noche*. Frankenstein, like Donoso's narrator, is a sick creator: he is in love with himself or with versions of himself, thereby compounding narcissism with incest; he creates out of season, in the fall, and he despises what he creates. The body that Frankenstein (the ultimate *bricoleur*) creates out of pieces taken from corpses seems to him beautiful as he creates it, yet becomes hideous when alive. Frankenstein at first flees it (represses its existence) when it comes to life and then spends the rest of his own life trying to destroy it. This antagonism between the creator and his creation may seem quite typical of romanticism, but it has further reaching ramifications. In Donoso's text, as in *Morel*, the conventional distinction between art and artist (the monster and Frankenstein) disappears, and the narrative itself is seen as a monstrous creator, incapable of doing anything except narrating, creating stories in its own image.

What the narrator (he has several names, but we see him first as the convent janitor, Mudito, the mute) says is in effect irrelevant. What matters most is the telling itself, the imposition of order (grammar) on arbitrarily chosen things (signs), and the equally arbitrary identification of certain segments of the discourse with certain names, and other parts with other names. The teller here is what he tells; the constant shifts of identity, of enclosure, are therefore nothing more or less than the ebb and flow of the discourse itself. It is always *in medias res*, wherever it happens to be, and it always ends with a death, a loss of voice. The final scene of *El obsceno pájaro de la noche* is one of total dispersion: a crone (a witch? a sybil?) empties over a fire, which consumes everything, the sack in which the narrator (by now nothing more than a disembodied voice) has been sewn: "In a few minutes nothing remains under the bridge. Only the black spot the fire left on the rocks and a blackened tin can with a wire handle. The wind knocks it over, it rolls along the rocks and falls into the river" (pp. 542–43/438).[3] The speaking mute (the text) is destroyed, just as it is in *Cien años de soledad*, but here there is no idea that a prophesy has been fulfilled, only the notion that the only death of the text, of the narrator/narrative, is silence.

To tell "what happens" in *El obsceno pájaro de la noche* is virtually impossible, and here again the text's huge size (some 530 pages in the original) and lack of a single unifying plot are signs of its monstrous nature. But a number of its stories may be listed: First (in reading, not chronological sequence) there is the story of the funeral of an old serving woman (Brígida) who lived in the Casa. This tale, narrated by Mudito, introduces the theme of death both as a starting point and as an end point for a narrative, the death-to-life of the author, his passing into the Arcadian immortality of literature, the theme of class relationships (especially between masters and servants), and the theme of enclosure (the convent, coffin, and vehicles). A second story, also set in the convent, is that of a perverse Immaculate Conception. One of the orphan girls in the convent has sexual relations with the narrator, who must wear a gigantic papier-mâché head to arouse her, and the old crones immediately define her pregnancy as a miracle. By verbal magic, the narrator becomes the miraculous child, becomes his own father.

The world inside the convent might have been described to provide an ironic contrast with the "real" world (like the contrast between hierarchies inside and outside of the military school in Mario Vargas Llosa's *La ciudad y los perros*),[4] but this is not so. The world outside the convent is no less an enclosure than the convent itself; there the enclosures are social classes, history, sexual roles, and education. Outside the convent (in an earlier period), the narrator becomes Humberto Peñaloza, sometime writer and factotum for the aristocratic Jerónimo de Azcoitía. Just as Mudito must wear a giant head in order to possess the orphan girl, Humberto can only possess his master's wife (Inés) by pretending to be his master. The product of that union is a monster, Boy, for whom his putative father, Jerónimo, builds a hidden world, populated only by monsters. Just as the narrative voice blends with the "miraculous" child in the convent, only to be engulfed by that world (in the form of the final crone), Jerónimo too is murdered by the world of freaks he creates, murdered by his own monstrous son. World-within-world, sphere-within-sphere, inside and outside: these pairs and oppositions are all states in which the narrative happens to find itself as it attempts to proliferate and survive. But none constitutes "reality" as such. They are all metaphors one for another, repetitions strung together until the fates (the convent crones?) cut the cord and nothing is left but a burned-out, empty can (enclosure) which falls into the river.

Any description of *El obsceno pájaro de la noche* is partial and therefore misleading, but it may also be stated that any one scene or story may be seen as a metaphor for any other scene or story, recalling once again the Ptolomaic system. Perhaps the one image that gives a kind of unity to the entire text (along with the package or enclosure motif) is the idea of the book itself. A book is a repository, an enclosure, in which signs, the doubly metaphoric marks which represent the oral signs, are deployed in a certain way. In Donoso's book the signs are arranged in the manner of the Ptolomaic system or, to use another analogy, a color wheel. We know that the color wheel represents the visible spectrum, the colors evoked in the eye by light stimulation. We do not see light in itself, but we do see its variations. The narrative in Donoso's text might be the equivalent of light: we experience it as a series of stories, some of which comment on the totality. The life of the narrative depends on the weaving of more and more variations, or on the repetition of those variations.

But built into the proliferation is the idea of death or ending. And this knowledge pervades the entire narrative. To write is to die, to continue to write is to draw nearer and nearer to the fatal moment, but to cease to write is also to die. It is for this reason the narrator is a crazed Proteus; he changes shape to prolong his life. He creates and discards names (his own and others) as he sees fit, but there is the maddening awareness in him that he will be appropriated, his identity taken by another, as he takes the identities of others. The narrative engenders the monsters which populate the text and which are the narrative, but those stories have their own order. The narrative is always threatened by one of its parts; the subplot may swallow up the main plot. In the same way, the act of publishing a book makes the author's name public property (as it is in "Borges and I"), and that act may constitute a loss of identity, a death. This problem is taken up in chapter 9, where Mudito/Humberto is caught trying to steal his own book from Jerónimo de Azcoitía's library, a vain attempt to recover his lost name.

The importance ascribed to names—the author's, the narrator's, the characters'—is of course illusory. Just as the reader suspects that the secret power in the text is actually the old women in the convent, who are nameless and who may very well be the outward manifestations of language, the signs, so also he wonders how a narrative voice as weak and fallible as that of Mudito/Humberto can really be generating the various stories. The end of the text would seem to bear this out because the crone who destroys the narrative voice by fire and leaves the blackened container for the wind to blow into the river is like a devil, like Mephistopheles come to claim Faust's soul. The narrative must be effaced, the deployed words returned to the lexicon, the narrative voice wiped out.

In no other of the satires considered in this study is the satirist so roundly satirized. To attempt to make oneself the master of language, to make oneself into the all-powerful Proteus, is impossible. The author is at best a partial Proteus, predestined like Kafka's hunger artist to do that which constitutes a slow sort of suicide; yet he cannot do otherwise. Donoso's text dramatizes the problem of the artist as only satire can: the artist is not a personality but a function, not a human being but an activity. It is not who but what the narrator is that is at stake here, just as it is in virtually all the works we have been examining. Machado's mad narrators leave texts that justify their meaningless lives; Bioy's anonymous diarist shows how the literary character becomes a text; Cortázar's Oliveira is nothing more than a plot seeking its resolution; Cabrera Infante's figures are nothing more than the pale transcriptions of an author/character, and so on. It is from language these texts come and to it they return. It fell to Donoso to delineate that trajectory in full, in its most tortuous and monstrous gyrations.

Epilogue

The provisional nature of this study must be recalled now as it ends. Most of the writers considered here are still productive; their work is in progress, subject to change without notice, innocent of the critic's strictures or schema. What has been postulated here is a means to grasp the situation of Latin American narrative fiction as an entity, to derive a theory of Latin American satire or romance which does not deform the individual text while it shows that text to be part of a homogeneous totality. The study is therefore limited. It in no way pretends to be complete in its coverage of all Latin American authors—an impossibility, since so much writing is being published throughout Latin America.

A study of literary genres will strike many readers of Latin American fiction as old fashioned or superfluous. Why worry about names—which is what genre designations are after all—when there is the text itself to consider? To this Aristotelian or, in Medieval terms, nominalist *reductus ad absurdam* there can be no real rejoinder except to say that a world, like that of Borges's Funes, in which every object has its own name, is a chaos. We may leave the "Asiatic disorder" to the real world, but in dealing with literature we must eventually come to grips with the similarities and differences of the objects under scrutiny. The relationship between the texts considered in this essay and the culture that produced them is not, despite the critical approach used here, a matter to be treated lightly. Dispersion has always plagued Latin America; perhaps finding the common elements of its fiction may help to show other common elements. Literary criticism, like its subject, is a part of culture, a part of human society, and it must inevitably return to that society to have significance.

This is by no means an attempt to debunk formalist approaches or to advocate a return to the techniques of Hippolyte Taine. It means simply that literary analysis is related to the study of particular societies and that literary analysis which precludes all connection of the literary text to culture in general is a sterile exercise. Not every experiment need, on the other hand, make a cultural point, but the possibility of seeing literary artifacts as the products of a culture must not be destroyed. This essay has attempted to provide a rhetorical means of linking literary texts from various cultures and periods—but all originating in that geographic zone we call Latin America—in order to show one aspect of the cultural unity of Latin America itself.

Notes

Introduction

1   For a definition of Latin America's colonial status see Stanley J. Stein and Barbara H. Stein, *The Colonial Heritage of Latin America: Essays on Economic Dependence in Perspective* (New York: Oxford University Press, 1970).

2   Borges's name reappears throughout this essay, although there is no chapter dedicated to him. His oeuvre taken as a whole resembles, in its encyclopedic scope, many of the texts studied here, but to analyze it thoroughly would require a separate book.

3   William K. Wimsatt, Jr., in "Comments to Part Nine," in *Style in Language,* ed. Thomas A. Sebeok (Cambridge, Mass.: M.I.T. Press, 1966), p. 422.

4   The two texts which will be most frequently cited here are the following: E. D. Hirsch, Jr., *Validity in Interpretation* (New Haven: Yale University Press, 1971); this text will be referred to as Hirsch. And Northrop Frye, *Anatomy of Criti-*

cism: Four Essays (Princeton: Princeton University Press, 1965); this text will be referred to as Frye.

5   Roman Jakobson and Morris Halle, *Fundamentals of Language,* 2d ed. (The Hague: Mouton, 1971). This matter is pursued in greater detail in chapter 1, below.

6   See particularly Georg Lukács, *The Historical Novel* (1937; Boston: Beacon Press, 1963). Of relevance to this study is the chapter "The Classical Form of the Historical Novel," with its interesting discussion of Sir Walter Scott.

7   James Olney, *Metaphors of Self: The Meaning of Autobiography* (Princeton: Princeton University Press, 1972).

8   Georg Lukács, "The Problems of a Philosophy of the History of Forms," in *The Theory of the Novel: A Historico-Philosophical Essay on the Forms of Great Epic Literature* (1920; London: Merlin Press, 1971), p. 41.

9   The best introduction to the historical phenomenon of the "Boom" is Emir Rodríguez Monegal, *El Boom de la novela latino-americana* (Caracas: Editorial Tiempo Nuevo, 1972).

10 See my *El individuo y el otro: Crítica a los cuentos de Julio Cortázar* (Buenos Aires: Ediciones La Librería, 1971), p. 15 ff.

11 See my "Cortázar 'novelista,'" *Mundo nuevo,* no. 18 (December 1967), pp. 38–42.

12 For a definition of satire comple-

mentary to Frye's, see Alvin B. Kernan, "Satire," *Dictionary of the History of Ideas*, ed. Philip W. Wiener (New York: Charles Scribner's Sons, 1973), 4:211–17.

Chapter 1

1   Ferdinand de Saussure, *Course in General Linguistics*, eds. Charles Bally and Albert Sechehaye, trans. Wade Baskin (New York: McGraw-Hill Book Co., 1966). See chapter 3, "Static and Evolutionary Linguistics."

2   *Memórias Póstumas de Brás Cubas*, in *Obra Completa*, ed. Afranio Coutinho (Rio de Janeiro: Editora José Aguilar, 1962), vol. 1; trans. by William L. Grossman, *Epitaph of a Small Winner* (New York: Noonday Press, 1972).

All quotations from the works discussed are translated by myself from the original-language editions cited. When there are published English translations of the work, one of these is also cited, and page references, when given, are to both versions. Pages in the original-language edition are given first, before a solidus; pages in the translation are given after the solidus.

3   This problem is studied below in different terms; see chap. 3.

4   See my "Rereading *Ressurreição*," *Luso-Brazilian Review* 9, no. 2 (winter 1972), pp. 47–57.

5   It might be noted that Sainte-Beuve, in a preface to de Maistre's text that Machado may have known, associates de Maistre with Sterne and Charles Lamb:

"Le Comte Xavier de Maistre," in
Voyage autour de ma chambre (1839;
Paris: Calmann Lévy, 1884), es-
pecially pp. 12–13.

6   Jorge Luis Borges, "Borges y yo,"
in *El Hacedor* (1960), vol. 9 of
Obras Completas (Buenos Aires:
Emecé Editores, 1967), pp. 50–51;
trans. by James E. Irby, "Borges
and I," in Donald A. Yates and
James E. Irby, eds., *Labyrinths*
(New York: New Directions,
1964), pp. 246–47.

Chapter 2   1   Jean-Jacques Rousseau, *The Confessions*, trans. J. M. Cohen (Lon-
don: Penguin Books, 1971), p. 88.

2   *Dom Casmurro*, in *Obra Completa*,
vol. 1; trans. by Helen Caldwell,
Dom Casmurro (Berkeley and Los
Angeles: University of California
Press, 1966).

3   See Arthur C. Danto, "Substan-
tive and Analytical Philosophy of
History," in *Analytical Philosophy
of History* (Cambridge: Cambridge
University Press, 1968), p. 11 ff.

Chapter 3   1   "El arte narrativo y la magia," in
Discusión, vol. 6 of *Obras Completas*
(Buenos Aires: Emecé Editores,
1966), p. 91; trans. by Norman
Thomas di Giovanni, "Narrative
Art and Magic," in *TriQuarterly*,
no. 25 (fall 1972), *Prose for Borges*,
pp. 209–15.

2   All citations for *La invención de
Morel* (1940) are to the 6th ed.
(Buenos Aires: Emecé Editores,
1970), which contains the original
Preface (1940) by Jorge Luis
Borges; trans. by Ruth L. C.

Simms, *The Invention of Morel and Other Stories* (Austin: University of Texas Press, 1964).

3   André Breton, "Manifesto of Surrealism," in *Manifestoes of Surrealism,* trans. Richard Seaver and Helen R. Lane (Ann Arbor: University of Michigan Press, 1972), pp. 6–7.

4   Cortázar actually has one of the characters of his first published extended fiction, *Los premios* (Buenos Aires: Editorial Sudamericana, 1960), repeat Valéry's remark (p. 11). Trans. by Elaine Kerrigan, *The Winners* (New York: Pantheon Books, 1965), p. 3.

5   Quoted in Borges's preface to *Morel* (my translation).

6   Borges's wonderful essay on *Bouvard et Pecuchet* in *Discusión,* vol. 6 of *Obras Completas,* pp. 137–45, is illuminating in this sense, but, as usual, Borges is not particularly concerned with genre theory.

7   Jorge Luis Borges, "Tlön, Uqbar, Orbis Tertius," In *Ficciones (1935–1944)* (Buenos Aires: Ediciones Sur, 1944), pp. 11–37; trans. by James E. Irby, "Tlön, Uqbar, Orbis Tertius," in Yates and Irby, eds., *Labyrinths,* pp. 3–18.

Chapter 4   1   See for example his *Theory of the Novel:* "The epic and the novel, these two major forms of great epic literature, differ from one another not by their authors' fundamental intentions but by the given historico-philosophical realities with which the authors were confronted" (p. 56). This is indeed "early" Lukács, but he never severed fully the connection between the two genres, just as he never differentiated between novel, satire, and romance.

2　*Plan de evasión* (Buenos Aires: Editorial Galerna, 1969); trans. by Suzanne Jill Levine, *A Plan for Escape* (New York: E. P. Dutton, 1975).

3　Arthur Rimbaud, "Délires, II Alchimie du verbe," *Une saison en enfer* in *Oeuvres*, ed. Suzanne Bernard, 2d. ed. (Paris: Editions Garnier Frères, 1962), p. 228.

Chapter 5

1　Robert Hollander, *Allegory in Dante's "Commedia"* (Princeton: Princeton University Press, 1969), p. 25.

2　*De donde son los cantantes* (Mexico City: Joaquín Mortiz, 1965; trans. by Suzanne Jill Levine, *From Cuba with a Song,* in *Triple Cross* (New York: E. P. Dutton, 1972).

3　This matter is taken up in chapter 7.

4　Jacques Lacan, "Seminar on 'The Purloined Letter," trans. Jeffrey Mehlman, in *French Freud: Structural Studies in Psychoanalysis,* Yale French Studies, no. 48 (1972), p. 54.

5　Roberto González Echevarría, "Rehearsal for *Cobra,*" *Review 74: Focus on "Cobra"* 13 (winter 1974): 38.

Chapter 6

1　Buenos Aires: Editorial Sudamericana, 1963; trans. by Gregory Rabassa, *Hopscotch* (New York: New American Library, 1967).

2   There are several instances of this in the text: "But I don't want to write about Rocamadour, at least not today" (p. 28/21), or "When I'm done cutting my nails or finished my hair, or simply now that, while I'm writing, I hear a gurgle in my stomach" (p. 455/330).

3   See my *El individuo y el otro: Crítica a los cuentos de Julio Cortázar* (Buenos Aires: Ediciones La Librería, 1971), pp. 15–27. For a statement about the religious aspects of Cortázar's writings see my "La torre de Dánae," *Revista Iberoamericana*, nos. 84–85 (December 1973), pp. 457–89.

4   In particular "Notas sobre la novela contemporánea," *Realidad*, no. 8 (March–April 1948), pp. 240–46, and "Situación de la novela," *Cuadernos americanos*, no. 4 (July-August 1950), pp. 294–97.

5   Harold Bloom, *The Anxiety of Influence: A Theory of Poetry* (New York: Oxford University Press, 1973).

6   Jorge Luis Borges, "La paradoja de Apollinaire," *Anales de Buenos Aires*, no. 8 (August 1946), pp. 48–51.

7   *El Boom de la novela latinoamericana* (Caracas: Editorial Tiempo Nuevo, 1972), p. 15.

8   Julio Cortázar actually translated Robinson Crusoe: *Vida y extrañas y sorprendientes aventuras de Robinson Crusoe, Marino de York, escritas*

por él mismo (Buenos Aires: Viau, 1945).

9   Stanley E. Fish, "To the Reader," *Self-consuming Artifacts: The Experience of Seventeenth-Century Literature* (Berkeley and Los Angeles: University of California Press, 1974), p. 4.

10   Joseph Frank, "Spatial Form in Modern Literature," in *The Widening Gyre* (New Brunswick, N. J.: Rutgers University Press, 1963), p. 19.

11   This is particularly true of Juan Carlos Onetti. García Márquez assumes something else, namely, that the reader of *Cien años* has read not only his earlier works, but works by other Spanish American writers as well.

Chapter 7

1   Paul de Man, "The Rhetoric of Blindness: Jacques Derrida's Reading of Rousseau," in *Blindness and Insight* (New York: Oxford University Press, 1971), pp. 102–41. See especially p. 106.

2   John Updike, "Infante Terrible," *The New Yorker*, 29 January 1972, pp. 91–94.

3   Emir Rodríguez Monegal, "Structure and Meanings of *Three Trapped Tigers*," *Latin American Literary Review*, spring 1973, p. 20.

4   *Tres tristes tigres* (Barcelona: Editorial Seix Barral, 1968); trans. by Donald Gardner and Suzanne Jill Levine, *Three Trapped Tigers* (New York: Harper and Row, 1971). See also p. 408/442, a conversation between Cué and Silvestre. Silvestre

begins, "We aren't literary characters." To which Cué answers,
"And when you write down these
nocturnal adventures?"

5   This theme is dealt with in chapter
9.

6   See Emanuele Tesauro, *Il Cannochiale aristotelico* (Bologna: Gioseffo Longhi, 1675), p. 325.

7   J. Hillis Miller, *The Form of Victorian Fiction* (Notre Dame: University of Notre Dame Press,
1970), p. 5.

Chapter 8

1   "Seminar on 'The Purloined Letter,' " p. 45.

2   *Grande Sertão: Veredas*, 6th ed. (Rio
de Janeiro: José Olympio Editôra,
1968); trans. by James L. Taylor
and Harriet de Onís, *The Devil to
Pay in the Backlands* (New York:
Alfred A. Knopf, 1971).

3   G. S. Kirk and J. E. Raven, "Heraclitus of Ephesus," in *The Pre-
Socratic Philosophers* (Cambridge: Cambridge University
Press, 1963), p. 188. All Heraclitian quotations are taken from
this edition.

4   Augusto de Campos, "Um lance
de 'Dês' do *Grande Sertão*," in
Pedro Xisto, Augusto de Campos,
and Haroldo de Campos, *Guimarães Rosa em três dimensões* (São
Paulo: Conselho Estadual de Cultura, Comissão Estadual de Literatura, 1970), pp. 55–58.

Chapter 9

1   Frank Kermode's *The Sense of an
Ending: Studies in the Theory of
Fiction* (New York: Oxford Uni-

versity Press, 1967) elucidates many of the problems touched on here.

2   *Cien años de soledad* (Buenos Aires: Editorial Sudamericana, 1967); trans. by Gregory Rabassa, *One Hundred Years of Solitude* (New York: Avon Books, 1971).

3   Frye, *Anatomy of Criticism*, p. 318.

4   Jorge Luis Borges, "La postulación de la realidad," in *Discusión*.

5   Mikhail Mikhailovich Bakhtin, *Rabelais and his World*, trans. Helene Iswosky (Cambridge, Mass.: M.I.T. Press, 1968).

6   "But it is a measure of the greatest satirists (perhaps the greatest men) that they recognize their own involvement in the folly of human life and willingly see themselves as victims, in obscure ways, of their own art" (Robert C. Elliott, "The Satirist Satirized: Studies of the Great Misanthropes," in *The Power of Satire: Magic, Ritual, Art* [Princeton: Princeton University Press, 1970], p. 222).

Chapter 10

1   "Spatial Form in Modern Literature," in *The Widening Gyre*, p. 13.

2   Juan Rulfo, *Pedro Páramo*, 4th ed. (Mexico City: Fondo de Cultura Económica, 1963); trans. by Lysander Kemp, *Pedro Páramo* (New York: Grove Press, 1969).

Chapter 11

1   Aristotle, *Poetics*, trans. Gerald F. Else (Ann Arbor: University of Michigan Press, 1967), p. 32.

2   *La traición de Rita Hayworth*

(Buenos Aires: Editorial Jorge Alvarez, 1967); trans. by Suzanne Jill Levine, *Betrayed by Rita Hayworth* (New York: E. P. Dutton, 1971).

3 *Boquitas pintadas: Folletín* (Buenos Aires: Editorial Sudamericana, 1969); trans. by Suzanne Jill Levine, *Heartbreak Tango: A Serial* (New York: E. P. Dutton, 1975).

4 Claude Lévi-Strauss, "From Cyclical Structure in Myth to Serial Romance in Modern Fiction," trans. Petra Morrison, in *Sociology of Literature and Drama*, eds., Elizabeth and Tom Burns (London: Penguin Books, 1973), p. 212.

Chapter 12

1 *Tratados en La Habana: Ensayos críticos* (Santiago, Chile: Editorial Oribe, 1970), pp. 42–45.

2 *Paradiso* (Buenos Aires: Ediciones de la Flor, 1968); trans. by Gregory Rabassa, *Paradiso* (New York: Farrar, Straus and Giroux, 1974).

3 *Cemí* is a remarkably suggestive name. A cemí is an idol worshipped in pre-Columbian antiquity. The sound of the name conjures up such notions as *sema*, or sign, and semen, or seed. The poet's name combines the divine, the idea of linguistic signs, and the sexual. At the same time, Cemí may be a pun on "c'est moi," a joke involving both the idea of fictionalized autobiography and the poet's coming to self-awareness.

4 *La vida breve* (Buenos Aires: Editorial Sudamericana, 1950); trans. by Hortense Carpentier, *A Brief Life* (New York: Grossman, 1976).

5   In *Las armas secretas* (Buenos
    Aires: Editorial Sudamericana,
    1959); trans. by Paul Blackburn,
    "Blowup," in *End of the Game and
    Other Stories* (New York: Pan-
    theon, 1967).

6   See Georges Bataille, *Les larmes
    d'eros* (Paris: Jean-Jacques Pauvert
    Editeur, 1964).

Chapter 13

1   Wayne C. Booth, *The Rhetoric of
    Fiction* (Chicago: University of
    Chicago Press, 1961), p. 383.

2   A. Bartlett Giamatti, "Proteus Un-
    bound: Some Versions of the Sea
    God in the Renaissance," in *The
    Disciplines of Criticism,* ed. Peter
    Demetz, Thomas Greene, and
    Lowry Nelson, Jr. (New Haven:
    Yale University Press, 1968). I
    wish to express my indebtedness
    to Giamatti for the concept of Pro-
    teus as well as the distinctions
    between *vates* and *magus.*

3   *El obsceno pájaro de la noche* (Bar-
    celona: Editorial Seix Barral,
    1970); trans. by Hardie St. Martin
    and Leonard Mades, *The Obscene
    Bird of Night* (New York: Alfred
    A. Knopf, 1973).

4   Barcelona: Editorial Seix Barral,
    1962.

Bibliography

This bibliography is divided into three parts: the first consists of works by the authors or collections in which their works appear, along with selected critical material; the second part is composed of secondary material, including works by Latin American authors not studied in detail and collections of essays on Latin American literature; the third section is a list of English translations cited in the notes along with the original-language editions. The reader is reminded that all translations of quoted passages are mine and that the page references for the English-language editions are intended as a convenience for those reading the works in translation.

I. Authors—texts and criticism

Bioy Casares, Adolfo (b. 1914)
La invención de Morel (1940). 6th ed. Preface by Jorge Luis Borges. Buenos Aires: Emecé Editores, 1970.
Plan de evasión (1945). Buenos Aires: Editorial Galerna, 1969.

Criticism:

Borinsky, Alicia. *"Plan de evasión* de Adolfo Bioy Casares: La representación de la representación." Paper read at the 16th Congreso del Instituto Internacional de Literatura Iberoamericana, August 1973, at Michigan State University. Mimeographed.

Kovacci, Ofelia. *Adolfo Bioy Casares.* Buenos Aires: Ediciones Culturales Argentinas, Ministerio de Educación y Justicia, Dirección General de Cultura, 1963.

————. *Espacio y tiempo en la fantasía de Adolfo Bioy Casares.* Buenos Aires: Universidad de Buenos Aires, 1963.

Cabrera Infante, Guillermo (b. 1929)

"Epilogue for Late(nt) Readers." *Review 72* 4–5 (winter–spring 1971/ 72): 23–32.

Tres tristes tigres. Barcelona: Editorial Seix Barral, 1968.

Un oficio del siglo xx, by G. Caín. (pseud.). Selection, notes, prologue, and epilogue by Guillermo Cabrera Infante. Havana: Ediciones de la Revolución, 1963.

Criticism:

Levine, Suzanne Jill. "Three Trapped Tigers and a Cobra." *Modern Language Notes,* Hispanic Issue, 90, no. 2 (March 1975): 265–77.

Rodríguez Monegal, Emir. "Structure and Meanings of *Three Trapped Tigers." Latin American Literary Review,* spring 1973, pp. 19–35.

Updike, John. "Infante Terrible." *The New Yorker,* 29 January 1972, pp. 91–94.

Cortázar, Julio (b. 1914)

Las armas secretas. Buenos Aires: Editorial Sudamericana, 1959.

"Notas sobre la novela contemporánea." *Realidad,* no. 8 (March–April 1948), pp. 240–46.

Los premios. Buenos Aires: Editorial Sudamericana, 1960.

Rayuela. Buenos Aires: Editorial Sudamericana, 1963.

"Situación de la novela." Cuadernos americanos, no. 4 (July–August 1950), pp. 294–97.

Ultimo Round. Mexico City: Siglo Veintiuno Editores, 1969.

Vida y extrañas y sorprendientes aventuras de Robinson Crusoe, marino de York, escritas por él mismo (translation). Buenos Aires: Viau, 1945.

La vuelta al día en ochenta mundos. Mexico City: Siglo Veintiuno Editores, 1967.

Criticism

Arrigucci Júnior, Davi. *O Escorpião encalacrado.* São Paulo: Editora Perspectiva, 1973.

Christ, Ronald, ed. *Review 72: Focus on Julio Cortázar*, vol. 7 (winter 1972).

Curutchet, Juan Carlos. *Julio Cortázar, o la crítica de la razón pragmática.* Madrid: Editora Nacional, 1972.

Mac Adam, Alfred J. "Cortázar 'novelista.' " *Mundo nuevo*, no. 18 (December 1967), pp. 38–42.

————. *El individuo y el otro: Crítica a los cuentos de Julio Cortázar.* Buenos Aires: Ediciones La Librería, 1971.

————. "Rayuela." In *La novela hispanoamericana actual: Compilación de ensayos críticos.* Edited by Angel Flores and Raúl Silva Cáceres. Garden City, N.Y., and Spain: Las Américas Publishing Co., 1971.

Revista Iberoamericana 84–85 (December 1973). Issue devoted to Cortázar; includes previously unpublished material by Cortázar.

Donoso, José (b. 1924)

Historia personal del "boom." Barcelona: Anagrama, 1972.

El obsceno pájaro de la noche. Barcelona: Editorial Seix Barral, 1970.

Criticism

Christ, Ronald, ed. *Review 73: Donoso, The Obscene Bird of Night*, vol. 9 (fall 1973). Includes an interview with Donoso.

García Márquez, Gabriel (b. 1928)

Cien años de soledad. Buenos Aires: Editorial Sudamericana, 1967.

El coronel no tiene quien le escriba (1961). Mexico City: Ediciones ERA, 1966.

La Hojarasca (1955). Buenos Aires: Editorial Sudamericana, 1969.

La mala hora. Mexico City: Ediciones ERA, 1966. While the first edition of this text appeared in 1962, García Márquez considers the 1966 edition to be the true "first edition." See prefatory note to 1966 edition.

La novela en América Latina: Diálogo entre García Márquez y Mario Vargas Llosa. Lima: C. Milla Batres, 1968.

Criticism

Ludmer, Josefina. *Cien años de soledad: Una interpretación.* Buenos Aires: Editorial Tiempo Contemporáneo, 1972.

Martínez, Pedro Simón, ed. *Recopilación de textos sobre Gabriel García Márquez.* Havana: Centro de Investigaciones Literarias, Casa de las Américas, 1969.

Rodríguez Monegal, Emir. "Novedad y anacronismo de *Cien años de soledad.*" *Revista Nacional de Cultura* 185 (July–August–September 1968): 3–23.

Segre, Cesare. "Il tempo curvo di García Márquez." In *I segni e la critica*.
Torino: Giulio Einaudi Editore, 1969.

Guimarães Rosa, João (1908–67)
   Grande Sertão: Veredas (1956). 6th ed. Rio de Janeiro: José Oympio
   Editôra, 1968.

Criticism
Daniel, Mary L. *João Guimarães Rosa: Travessia literária*. Rio de Janeiro:
   José Olympio Editôra, 1968.
Galvão, Walnice Nogueira. *As Formas do falso: Um estudo sôbre a am-
   bigüidade no "Grande Sertão: Veredas."* São Paulo: Editôra Perspectiva,
   1972.
Xisto, Pedro; de Campos, Augusto; and de Campos, Haroldo.
   Guimarães Rosa em três dimensões. São Paulo: Conselho Estadual de
   Cultura, Comissão Estadual de Literatura, 1970.

Lezama Lima, José (b. 1910)
   "Complejo y complicado." In *Tratados en La Habana: Ensayos críticos*.
   Santiago, Chile: Editorial Oribe, 1970.
   Paradiso. Buenos Aires: Ediciones de la Flor, 1968.

Criticism
Cortázar, Julio. "Para llegar a Lezama Lima." In *La vuelta al día en
   ochenta mundos*. Mexico City: Siglo Veintiuno Editores, 1967.
Ortega, Julio. "*Paradiso*, de Lezama Lima." In *La Novela hispanoamericana
   actual*, edited by Angel Flores and Raúl Silva Cáceres. Garden City,
   N.Y., and Spain: Las Américas, 1971.
Martínez, Pedro Simón, ed. *Recopilación de textos sobre José Lezama Lima*.
   Havana: Casa de las Américas, 1970.
Sarduy, Severo. "Un Proust cubain." *La Quinzaine Littéraire* 15 (1971):
   3–4.

Machado de Assis, Joaquim Maria (1839–1908)
   Obra completa. Edited by Afranio Coutinho. 3 vols. Rio de Janeiro:
   Editôra José Aguilar, 1962. Contains *Dom Casmurro* (1899), *Memórias
   Póstumas de Brás Cubas* (1881), and *Ressurreiçâo* (1872).

Criticism
Caldwell, Helen. *The Brazilian Othello of Machado de Assis: A Study of
   "Dom Casmurro."* Perspectives in Criticism. Berkeley: University of
   California Press, 1960.
————. *Machado de Assis: The Brazilian Master and His Novels*. Berkeley:

University of California Press, 1970.
Gomes, Eugenio. *Machado de Assis*. Rio de Janeiro: Livraria São José, 1958.
————. *O enigma de Capitu: Ensaio de interpretação*. Rio de Janeiro: Livraria José Olympio Editôra, 1967.
Mac Adam, Alfred J. "Rereading *Ressurreição*." *Luso-Brazilian Review* 9, no. 2 (winter 1972): 47–57.
Magalhães, Raymundo. *Machado de Assis desconhecido*. 3d ed. Rio de Janeiro: Editôra Civilização Brasileira, 1957.
Massa, Jean Michele. "La jeunesse de Machado de Assis (1839–1870): Essai de biographie intellectuelle." 2 vols. Dissertation, Faculté des Lettres et Sciences Humaines de Poitiers, 1969.

Onetti, Juan Carlos (b. 1909)
La vida breve. Buenos Aires: Editorial Sudamericana, 1950.

Criticism
Ainsa, Fernando. *Las trampas de Onetti*. Montevideo: Editorial Arca, 1970.
Irby, James E. "Aspectos formales de *La vida breve* de Juan Carlos Onetti." In *Actas del Tercer Congreso Internacional de Hispanistas*. México: Colegio de México, 1970.
————. "La influencia de William Faulkner en cuatro narradores hispanoamericanos." Master's thesis, Universidad Autónoma de México, 1956.
García Ramos, Renaldo, ed. *Recopilición de textos sobre Juan Carlos Onetti*. Havana: Centro de Investigaciones Literarias, Casa de Las Américas, 1969.

Puig, Manuel (b. 1932)
La tración de Rita Hayworth. Buenos Aires: Editorial Jorge Alvarez, 1967.
Boquitas pintadas: Folletín. Buenos Aires: Editorial Sudamericana, 1969.

Criticism
Borinsky, Alicia. "Castración y lujos: La escritura de Manuel Puig." *Revista Iberoamericana* 41, no. 90 (January–March 1975): 29–45.
Mac Adam, Alfred J. "Manuel Puig's Chronicles of Provincial Life." *Revista Hispánica Moderna*, nos. 1–2 (1973): 50–65.
Sarduy, Severo. "Notas a las notas a las notas . . . : A propósito de Manuel Puig." *Revista Iberoamericana* 37, nos. 76–77 (July–December 1971): 555–67.

Rulfo, Juan (b. 1918)
Pedro Páramo (1955). 4th ed. Mexico City: Fondo de Cultura Económica, 1963.

Criticism

Irby, James E. *See entry under* Onetti.
Recopilación de textos sobre Juan Rulfo. Havana: Centro de Investigaciones Literarias, Casa de las Américas, 1969.

Sarduy, Severo (b. 1937)
De donde son los cantantes. Mexico City: Joaquín Mortíz, 1965.
Cobra. Buenos Aires: Editorial Sudamericana, 1972.
Escrito sobre un cuerpo: Ensayos de crítica. Buenos Aires: Editorial Sudamericana, 1969.

Criticism

Christ, Ronald, ed. *Review 72: Focus on Octavio Paz and Severo Sarduy.* 6 (fall 1972).
────, ed. *Review 74: Focus on "Cobra,"* vol. 13 (winter 1974).
González Echevarría, Roberto. "Són de La Habana: La ruta de Severo Sarduy." *Revista Iberoamericana.* 37, nos. 76–77 (July–December 1971): 725–40.

II. Secondary Material

Angenot, Marc. "The Classical Structure of the Novel: Remarks on Georg Lukács, Lucien Goldmann, and René Girard." *Genre.* 3, no. 3 (September 1970): 205–13.
Aristotle. *Poetics.* Translated by Gerald F. Else. Ann Arbor: University of Michigan Press, 1967.
Auerbach, Eric. *Mimesis: The Representation of Reality in Western Literature.* Translated by Willard Trask. New York: Doubleday, 1957.
Bakhtin, Mikhail Mikhailovich. *Rabelais and His World.* Translated by Helene Iswosky. Cambridge, Mass.: M.I.T. Press, 1968.
Barthes, Roland. *Le plaisir du texte.* Paris: Editions du Seuil, 1973.
────. *S/Z.* Translated by Richard Miller; Preface by Richard Howard. New York: Hill and Wang, 1974.
Bataille, Georges. *Death and Sensuality: A Study of Eroticism and the Taboo.* New York: Ballantine Books, 1969.
────. *Les larmes d'Eros.* Paris: Jean-Jacques Pauvert Editeur, 1964.
Bloom, Harold. *The Anxiety of Influence: A Theory of Poetry.* New York: Oxford University Press, 1973.
Borges, Jorge Luis. "Borges y yo." In *El hacedor* (1960), vol. 9 of *Obras completas.* Buenos Aires: Emecé Editores, 1967.

————. *Discusión* (1932). Vol. 6 of *Obras completas*. Buenos Aires: Emecé Editores, 1966.

————. *Ficciones (1935–1944)*. Buenos Aires: Ediciones Sur, 1944.

————. "La paradoja de Apollinaire." *Anales de Buenos Aires*, no. 8 (August 1946), pp. 48–51.

Breton, André. *Manifestoes of Surrealism*. Translated by Richard Seaver and Helen R. Lane. Ann Arbor: University of Michigan Press, 1972.

Burke, Kenneth. "Poetic Categories." In *Attitudes toward History*. Boston: Beacon Press, 1961.

Carpentier, Alejo. *El siglo de las luces*. México: Compañía General de Ediciones, 1962.

Coutinho, Afranio, ed. *A Literatura no Brasil*. 5 vols. 2d ed. Rio de Janeiro: Editorial Sul Americana, 1968–70.

Crane, R. S. "The Concept of Plot and the Plot of *Tom Jones*." In *Critics and Criticism*, abr. ed. Edited by R. S. Crane. Chicago: University of Chicago Press, 1957.

Curtius, Ernst Robert. *European Literature and the Latin Middle Ages*. Translated by Willard Trask. New York: Harper and Row, 1963.

Danto, Arthur C. *Analytical Philosophy of History*. Cambridge: Cambridge University Press, 1968.

Ducrot, Oswald, and Todorov, Tzvetan. *Dictionnaire encyclopédique des sciences du langue*. Paris: Editions du Seuil, 1972.

Elliott, Robert C. *The Power of Satire: Magic, Ritual, Art*. Princeton: Princeton University Press, 1970.

Erlich, Victor. *Russian Formalism: History-Doctrine*. 2d ed. The Hague: Mouton, 1965.

Fernández Retamar, Roberto. "Para una teoría de la literatura hispanoamericana." *Casa de las Américas* 80 (September–October 1973): 128–34.

Fish, Stanley E. *Self-Consuming Artifacts: The Experience of Seventeenth-Century Literature*. Berkeley and Los Angeles: University of California Press, 1974.

Frank, Joseph. *The Widening Gyre*. New Brunswick: Rutgers University Press, 1963.

Friedman, Alan. *The Turn of the Novel: The Transition to Modern Fiction*. New York: Oxford University Press, 1970.

Frye, Northrop. *Anatomy of Criticism: Four Essays*. Princeton: Princeton University Press, 1965.

Fuentes, Carlos. *La muerte de Artemio Cruz*. Mexico City: Fondo de Cultura Económica, 1962.

————. *La nueva novela hispanoamericana*. Mexico City: Joaquín Mortiz, 1969.

Giamatti, A. Bartlett. "Proteus Unbound: Some Versions of the Sea God in the Renaissance." In *The Disciplines of Criticism*, edited by Peter

Demetz, Thomas Greene, and Lowry Nelson, Jr. New Haven: Yale University Press, 1968.

Girard, René. *Deceit, Desire, and the Novel: Self and Other in Literary Structure.* Translated by Yvonne Freccero. Baltimore: Johns Hopkins Press, 1965.

————. *La Violence et le sacré.* Paris: Editions Bernard Grasset, 1972.

Goldmann, Lucien. *Pour une sociologie du roman.* Paris: Gallimard, 1964.

Gombrich, E. H. *Symbolic Images: Studies in the Art of the Renaissance.* London: Phaidon Press, 1972.

Guillén, Claudio. *Literature as System: Essays toward the Theory of Literary History.* Princeton: Princeton University Press, 1971.

Hegel, Georg Wilhelm Friedrich. *Estetica.* Edited by Niccolao Merker; translated by Niccolao Merker and Niccola Vaccaro. Milan: Giulio Einaudi Editore, 1967.

————. *The Philosophy of History.* Translated by J. Sibree; Introduction by C. J. Friedrich. New York: Dover Publications, 1956.

Heidegger, Martin. *Being and Time.* Translated by John Macquarrie and Edward Robinson. New York: Harper and Row, 1962.

Hemmings, F. W. J. *Emile Zola.* 2d ed. Oxford: Oxford University Press, 1970.

Highet, Gilbert. *The Anatomy of Satire.* Princeton: Princeton University Press, 1966.

Hillis Miller, J. *The Form of Victorian Fiction.* Notre Dame: University of Notre Dame Press, 1970.

Hirsch, E. D., Jr. *Validity in Interpretation.* New Haven: Yale University Press, 1971.

Hollander, Robert. *Allegory in Dante's "Commedia."* Princeton: Princeton University Press, 1969.

Jakobson, Roman, and Halle, Morris. *Fundamentals of Language.* 2d ed. The Hague: Mouton, 1971.

Kermode, Frank. *The Romantic Image.* New York: Vintage Books, 1964.

————. *The Sense of an Ending: Studies in the Theory of Fiction.* New York: Oxford University Press, 1967.

Kernan, Alvin B. *The Plot of Satire.* New Haven: Yale University Press, 1965.

————. "Satire." In *Dictionary of the History of Ideas: Studies of Selected Pivotal Ideas,* edited by Philip P. Wiener, 4:211–17. New York: Charles Scribner's Sons, 1973.

Kirk, G. S., and Raven, J. E. *The Pre-Socratic Philosophers.* Cambridge: Cambridge University Press, 1963.

Lacan, Jacques. "Seminar on 'The Purloined Letter.'" Translated by Jeffrey Mehlman. In *French Freud: Structural Studies in Psychoanalysis,* Yale French Studies, no. 48 (1972), pp. 39–72.

Lemon, Lee T. and Reis, Marion J. editors and translators. *Russian Formalist Criticism*. Regents Critics Series. Lincoln: University of Nebraska Press, 1965.

Lévi-Strauss, Claude. "From Cyclical Structure in Myth to Serial Romance in Modern Fiction." Translated by Petra Morrison. In *Sociology of Literature and Drama*, edited by Elizabeth and Tom Burns. London: Penguin Books, 1975.

Lukács, Georg. *The Historical Novel* (1937). Boston: Beacon Press, 1963.
————. *The Theory of the Novel* (1920). London: Merlin Press, 1971.

Macksey, Richard, and Donato, Eugenio, eds. *The Structuralist Controversy: The Languages of Criticism and the Sciences of Man*. Baltimore: Johns Hopkins Press, 1972.

MacQueen, John. *Allegory, The Critical Idiom*. London: Methuen, 1970.

de Man, Paul. *Blindness and Insight*. New York: Oxford University Press, 1971.

Mendilow, A. A. *Time and the Novel*. Introduction by Professor J. Isaacs. New York: Humanities Press, 1972.

Olney, James. *Metaphors of Self: The Meaning of Autobiography*. Princeton: Princeton University Press, 1972.

Ortega, Julio. *La contemplación y la fiesta: Notas sobre la novela latinoamericana actual*. Caracas: Monte Avila Editores, 1969.

Paulson, Ronald. *The Fictions of Satire*. Baltimore: Johns Hopkins Press, 1967.

Pollard, Arthur. *Satire, The Critical Idiom*. London: Methuen, 1970.

Praz, Mario. *The Romantic Agony*. Translated by Angus Davidson. Cleveland: World Publishing Co., 1965.

Reeve, Clara. *The Progress of Romance through Times, Countries, and Manners; with Remarks on the Good and Bad Effects of It, on Them Respectively; in a Course of Evening Conversations*. England: W. Keymer, 1785.

Rimbaud, Arthur. *Oeuvres*. Edited by Suzanne Bernard. 2d ed. Paris: Editions Garnier Frères, 1962.

Rodríguez Monegal, Emir. *El Boom de la novela latinoamericana*. Caracas: Editorial Tiempo Nuevo, 1972.
————. *Narradores de esta América*. 2 vols. Montevideo and Buenos Aires: Editorial Alfa, 1969 and 1974.

Rousseau, Jean-Jacques. *The Confessions*. Translated by J. M. Cohen. London: Penguin Books, 1971.

Sainte-Beuve, Charles-Augustin. "Le comte Xavier de Maistre." In *Voyage autour de ma chambre*. Paris: Calmann Lévy, 1884.

de Saussure, Ferdinand. *Course in General Linguistics*. Edited by Charles Bally and Albert Sechehaye. Translated by Wade Baskin. New York: McGraw-Hill, 1966.

Scholes, Robert, and Kellog, Robert. *The Nature of Narrative*. New York:

Oxford University Press, 1971.

Souza, Antonio Cândido Mello e. *Vários escritos*. São Paulo: Livraria Duas Cidades, 1970.

Stein, Stanley J., and Stein, Barbara H. *The Colonial Heritage of Latin America: Essays on Economic Dependence in Perspective*. New York: Oxford University Press, 1970.

Stevick, Philip, ed. *The Theory of the Novel*. New York: Free Press, 1967.

Tesauro, Emanuele. *Il Cannochiale aristotelico*. Bologna: Gioseffo Longhi, 1675.

Vargas Llosa, Mario. *La ciudad y los perros*. Barcelona: Editorial Seix Barral, 1962.

Vivas, Eliseo. "Literary Classes: Some Problems." *Genre* 1, no. 2 (April 1968): 97–105.

Watt, Ian. *The Rise of the Novel: Studies in Defoe, Richardson, and Fielding*. Berkeley: University of California Press, 1967.

Weinberg, Bernard. *A History of Literary Criticism in the Italian Renaissance*. 2 vols. Chicago: University of Chicago Press, 1963.

Wellek, René, and Warren, Austin. *Theory of Literature*. 3d ed. New York: Harcourt, Brace, and World, 1962.

Wimsatt, William, Jr. "Comments to Part Nine." In *Style and Language*. Edited by Thomas A. Sebeok. Cambridge, Mass.: M.I.T. Press, 1966.

Wimsatt, William, Jr., and Brooks, Cleanth. *Literary Criticism: A Short History*. New York: Vintage Books, 1957.

III. English Translations of Latin American Texts Cited

Bioy Casares, Adolfo. *The Invention of Morel and Other Stories*. Preface by Jorge Luis Borges. Translated by Ruth L. C. Simms. Austin: University of Texas Press, 1964.

———. *A Plan for Escape*. Translated by Suzanne Jill Levine. New York: E. P. Dutton, 1975.

Borges, Jorge Luis. "Borges and I." In *Labyrinths*, edited by Donald A. Yates and James E. Irby. Translated by James E. Irby. New York: New Directions, 1964.

———. "Narrative Art and Magic." Translated by Norman Thomas di Giovanni. In *TriQuarterly*, no. 25 (fall 1972), *Prose for Borges*, edited by Mary Kinzie, pp. 209–15.

———. "Preface" to *The Invention of Morel*. See Bioy Casares.

———. "Tlön, Uqbar, Orbis Tertius." Translated by James E. Irby. In *Labyrinths*, edited by Donald A. Yates and James E. Irby. New York: New Directions, 1964.

Cabrera Infante, Guillermo. *Three Trapped Tigers*. Translated by Donald Gardner and Suzanne Jill Levine. New York: Harper and Row, 1971.

Cortázar, Julio. "Blowup." In *End of the Game and Other Stories*, translated by Paul Blackburn. New York: Pantheon Books, 1967.

———. *Hopscotch*. Translated by Gregory Rabassa. New York: New American Library, 1967.

———. *The Winners*. Translated by Elaine Kerrigan. New York: Pantheon Books, 1965.

Donoso, José. *The Obscene Bird of Night*. Translated by Hardie St. Martin and Leonard Mades. New York: Alfred A. Knopf, 1973.

García Márquez, Gabriel. *One Hundred Years of Solitude*. Translated by Gregory Rabassa. New York: Avon Books, 1971.

Guimarães Rosa, João. *The Devil to Pay in the Backlands*. Translated by James L. Taylor and Harriet de Onís. New York: Alfred A. Knopf, 1971.

Lezama Lima, José. *Paradiso*. Translated by Gregory Rabassa. New York: Farrar, Straus and Giroux, 1974.

Machado de Assis, Joaquim Maria. *Dom Casmurro*. Translated by Helen Caldwell. Berkely and Los Angeles: University of California Press, 1966.

———. *Epitaph of a Small Winner*. Translated by William L. Grossman. New York: Noonday Press, 1972.

Onetti, Juan Carlos. *A Brief Life*. Translated by Hortense Carpentier. New York: Grossman, 1976.

Puig, Manuel. *Betrayed by Rita Hayworth*. Translated by Suzanne Jill Levine. New York: E. P. Dutton, 1971.

———. *Heartbreak Tango: A Serial*. Translated by Suzanne Jill Levine. New York: E. P. Dutton, 1975.

Rulfo, Juan. *Pedro Páramo*. Translated by Lysander Kemp. New York: Grove Press, 1969.

Sarduy, Severo. *From Cuba with a Song*. In *Triple Cross*, translated by Suzanne Jill Levine. New York: E. P. Dutton, 1972.

Index